HINTERLAND

G000147182

Hinterland offers ~~~~~
question 'what is ~~~~~
by showcasing the ~~~~~
the fields of memoi~~~~~
food writing, repor~~~~~
biography, flash non-fiction and more.

Our pages bring together work by
established, award-winning authors
alongside new writers, many of whom
we are thrilled to publish for the first time
and whose work, we promise, will merit
your full attention.

Often, the pieces you'll find in Hinterland
will straddle the boundaries between
strands and be difficult to classify:
we see this as a strength. Hinterland
intends to challenge, move, entertain
and, above all, be a fantastic read.

WELCOME TO ISSUE 3

Advocates for Hinterland:
Trevor Goul-Wheeker, Nathan Hamilton, Rachel Hore,
Kathryn Hughes, Helen Smith, Rebecca Stott, Ian Thomson

Editorial Team
Editors-In-Chief – Freya Dean & Andrew Kenrick
Art Direction & Design – Tom Hutchings
Business Support – Ben Watkins
Readers – Susan K Burton, Aaron Deary, Margaret Hedderman,
Yin F Lim, Aaron O'Farrell, Stephen Massil

Submissions
Hinterland is committed to paying writers and artists for all work we publish.
Please send us your work via Submittable:
hinterlandnonfiction.submittable.com
We accept submissions year-round and endeavour to reply within 4 months.
We regret we are unable to provide feedback.
There is a small fee of £3 per submission.

Subscriptions
An annual subscription to Hinterland
(four issues, print and digital) costs £34 U.K.,
£44 Europe, £54 Rest-of-world.
Digital subscription only, £20.
Please visit our website for full details.

Distribution
Hinterland is distributed worldwide by NBN International.
For all trade orders contact +44 (0) 1752 202301
orders@nbninternational.com

Advertising
Please see our website for current rates, or to discuss sponsorship please
contact us at hinterlandnonfiction@gmail.com

Acknowledgments
The Editors gratefully acknowledge financial contributions from the UEA
Enterprise Santander fund and support from the UEA Publishing Project.

Find Hinterland online at
www.hinterlandnonfiction.com
or contact us: hinterlandnonfiction@gmail.com

ISBN: 978-1-911343-87-5
ISSN (Print): 2632-136X
ISSN (Online): 2632-1378

Copyright is reserved to the authors and artists, their heirs and executors.
All other text is copyright Hinterland Press Ltd. Hinterland is a registered
trademark of Hinterland Press Ltd. Hinterland Press Ltd is a registered company in
England and Wales, company number #11726436.

HINTERLAND®

THE BEST NEW CREATIVE NON-FICTION

Issue 3
AUTUMN
2019

Issue 3 / Autumn 2019

Editorial

Welcome to this autumnal issue of Hinterland in which, among an already stellar line up of writing talent, we present the three winners of The Hinterland Prize 2019. The idea for a prize for creative non-fiction came about in the earliest stages of planning for the launch of Hinterland itself. We saw it as another way to unearth work by emerging, as-yet-unpublished writers – those who, without a publication record, might ordinarily hesitate to submit their work to a magazine but who, within the framework of a prize, would hopefully feel emboldened to do so. We were thrilled to see that prize submissions came as much from 'new' writers as those who already had work in print. So many of the entries arrived like a gift: fresh, distinct voices that really struck out from the page and commanded our complete attention.

The winning three pieces are to be celebrated as wonderful examples of this 'must-read' quality; and it is with huge pleasure that we publish them in their entirety within the pages of this issue. *Sew Me A Song* by Anna Lachkaya is our overall winner and will be Anna's first published work. This is astonishing

Freya Dean is of Dutch-British descent. She was an Elizabeth Kostova Foundation Finalist in 2017 and the recipient of the 2017/2018 Lorna Sage Award. Her work has appeared in *Visual Verse*, *The Writes of Woman* and *UEA's NonFiction Anthology*.

given what a controlled, rich story it is. The judges were unanimous in selecting it as overall winner. *Snake Pass* by Megan Holland is awarded second place; a remarkable articulation of grief, love and our need to belong, made highly accessible through the narrator's voice. *Remembering Ice* by Dani Redd is our third-placed winner. The kind of hybrid piece that we love to read, it blends memoir, literary criticism and a psychoscape-like roam across a remote island, and was celebrated for being the most original in its approach.

The prize was judged by Euan Thorneycroft of literary agency A.M. Heath; with all shortlisted entries also valuably reviewed by our peer review panel, drawn from recent alumni of UEA's Creative Writing programs: Susan Karen Burton, Peter Goulding and Yin Lim. Our huge thanks to all those involved – and above all to the very many of you who submitted a piece for consideration. And please remember, no need to wait until next year to submit to us: our regular submissions platform is always open on Submittable (see page 14).

Happy reading.

Andrew Kenrick has worked as an archaeologist and an archivist, a writer and an editor. He is currently studying for a PhD at the University of East Anglia, where he is researching new ways to write biographies of ancient figures.

Contributors

Bella Braxton (*How to do the Job*) is a sophomore at Agnes Scott College. She lives in Atlanta, Georgia and works at a grocery store.

Margaret O'Brien (*Suppose I Were to Begin*) co-founded The Story House Ireland and is an affiliate of Amherst Writers & Artists. She curates the annual Brewery Lane Writers' weekend and runs the monthly open mic, Poetry Plus, alongside the workshop series Writing Changes Lives, in Brewery Lane Theatre, Carrick-on-Suir. Previously Margaret lectured in English and Creative Writing at Waterford Institute of Technology. Her work has been published by *Southword*, *The South Circular*, *RTE/O'Brien Press*, *Flash Frontier*, *The Pickled Body* and *The Irish Times*.

Steve Cushman (*Collectors*) earned an MFA from UNC-Greensboro and has published three novels. His poetry collection, *How Birds Fly*, won the 2018 Lena Shull Book Award.

Amy Davies (*Thank You, Penarth*) is a journalist and photographer. She is the Features Editor for *Amateur Photographer*, Britain's oldest weekly photography magazine, as well as contributing freelance articles to a wide range of different titles. Although English, she lives in Cardiff, South Wales, with her long-suffering sausage dog, Lola.

Michael Fischer (*Lights, Camera*) is a Moth StorySlam winner, a Luminarts Cultural Foundation Fellow, and a mentor for incarcerated authors through the Pen City Writers program. His work appears in *Salon*, *The Sun*, *Orion*, *Guernica*, *The Rumpus* and elsewhere; and his audio essays have been broadcast on CBC Radio's 'Love Me' and *The New York Times's* 'Modern Love: The Podcast.'

Megan Holland (*The Snake Pass*) writes across multiple genres and platforms. A short story, *The Coalman*, raised funds for the homeless charity Barnabus; while her novel *The Last Picture House* was selected for the Penguin Random House initiative Writenow. *Resistance*, a play, was performed at Oldham Coliseum Theatre as part of the First Break festival and another short story, *Date Night*, won the Creative Future Literary Awards 2017. Megan is also being mentored by the LGBTQ initiative Raising Our Voices.

Emily Holt's (*Restless Creature*) first poetry collection, *Though the Walls Are Lit*, is forthcoming in 2020 from Lost Horse Press. She received an MFA from the Rainier Writing Workshop at Pacific Lutheran University and a Master of Letters in Literature from Trinity College University of Dublin. She lives in Seattle, Washington.

Tom Hutchings is our in-house graphic designer and photographer, based in the south of London. As a new father, Tom is enjoying a lot of tummy time and finding out how delicious fingers are. Have a look at his varied output at www.thorngraphicdesign.com.

Mark Anthony Jarman's (*The Crooked Grocer*) short stories and non-fiction have been published in Europe and North America and he is a fiction editor for *The Fiddlehead* literary journal in Canada. His most recent book is *Knife Party at the Hotel Europa*.

Chris Jennings (*Starting Salary*) is an author and technologist in the San Francisco Bay Area who has co-authored a number of academic publications and is contributing editor to several e-learning magazines. His non-fiction has appeared in *daCunha*. Chris has a BA in Creative Writing and Masters degrees in both American Studies and Interactive Telecommunications. In addition to writing, Chris works at Google where he designs free online learning programs and delivery platforms used by over a million people worldwide.

Anna Lachkaya (*Sew Me a Song*) is a Faculty-Led Programs Coordinator at Agnes Scott College, where she organizes global learning trips. Her passion for writing and learning remains strong both personally and professionally. Anna grew up in Riga, Latvia and currently lives in Atlanta, Georgia with her husband and two sons.

Christopher Linforth (*Undersigned*) has published work in *Notre Dame Review*, *Fiction International*, *The Millions*, *South Dakota Review* and other literary magazines.

Andrew Menard (*Sons of Neptune*) is the author of two books: a monograph on the nineteenth-century American explorer John Frémont and a literary non-fiction account of Henry David Thoreau. Articles and essays have appeared in everything from *Artforum*, *Studio International* and *Oxford Art Journal* to *The New England Quarterly*, *Georgia Review* and *Antioch Review*.

Rebecca Pymar (*The British Library*) is an artist living and working in Norwich. Her work focuses on the built environment, illustrating places and spaces which have history and meaning. Rebecca's style is stripped back, stylised and precise, paying close attention to both colour and perspective; creating balanced yet striking pieces. She is inspired by what she sees around her and adopts a minimal approach to colour and detail, focusing on form and composition to create instantly recognisable and memorable pieces.

Dani Redd (*Remembering Ice*) has a PhD in Creative and Critical Writing from UEA. She writes both fiction and non-fiction, with work appearing in *National Geographic Traveller India, Words and Women, Herizons, The Island Review* and many more. Much of her writing is devoted to exploring the topographies and cultures of remote islands. She is currently working on a novel entitled *The Arctic Curry Club*, set between Spitsbergen and Bangalore, India, a city where she lived for two years.

Kimmo Rosenthal (*Helvetia*) has been teaching mathematics for over three decades. In the last half-dozen years he has turned his attention from mathematical research to writing. His work has appeared in *Prime Number* (nominated for a Pushcart Prize), *EDGE, decomP, KYSO Flash, The Fib Review*, and *The Ekphrastic Review*.

George Szirtes (*At the Ambassadors, In Conversation with*) was born in Hungary in 1948. His first book, *The Slant Door* (1979) won the Faber Prize. He has published many since then, Reel (2004) winning the T.S. Eliot Prize, for which he has been twice shortlisted since. His memoir, The *Photographer at Sixteen*, was published in February 2019.

Helen Szirtes (*In Conversation with*) spent several years as an editor at Bloomsbury Publishing in London before going freelance in 2008. She has worked on books by many notable authors, including Sarah Crossan, Caoilin Hughes, Philip Reeve, Alexander McCall Smith and JK Rowling. With her partner, designer and illustrator Richard Horne, she coauthored the bestselling *101 Things To Do Before You're Old and Boring*. Helen continues to edit and write for children from her home in Norwich.

René Georg Vasicek (*Notes from a Czechoslovakian Machine Shop*) is the author of *The Defectors* (forthcoming 2020, J.New Books). He earned an MFA at Sarah Lawrence College and was awarded an NEA fellowship. His work has appeared, or is forthcoming, in *Gargoyle*, *Barrelhouse*, *Mid-American Review*, *Post Road*, *Wigleaf* and elsewhere. He lives in New York City.

HINTERLAND

At Hinterland we are committed to publishing the best in creative non-fiction from around the globe.

We are always thrilled to feature work from established, well-known authors but have a particular interest in discovering new voices and in pieces that sit outside the usual categories: we ask only that it be a work of non-fiction.

We operate an open, year-round submissions policy and aim to read all work submitted within three months.

We pay for all the work that we publish and receive frequent interest from agents and publishers regarding our contributors.

Please send us your best work and we will endeavour to find a place for it.

Guidelines for submissions

- Submissions should be made via Submittable only. Please follow the link below:

- A small fee of £3 per submission applies to non-subscribers. Subscribers enjoy the benefit of submitting their work for free.

- All work should be new, previously unpublished material. If your work is subsequently accepted elsewhere, please kindly let us know.

- Pieces should not run to more than 5000 words. We accept anything from 500 words (very short pieces will be considered for our flash non-fiction slot). We also accept extracts from longer works, or works in progress.

- We warmly embrace writing on any topic, or from any genre, we ask only that it falls somewhere in the realm of non-fiction writing.

- Your work will be considered for all upcoming issues; it might help you to know that we operate a 3-4 month editorial lead time.

- We regret that, due to the number of submissions received, we cannot provide feedback.

hinterland.submittable.com/submit

Lights, Camera

Michael Fischer

My mom takes me to visit him on set. I walk
through the huge bay doors, the interior cavernous
as an airplane hangar. It's filled with full-size fake
living rooms, fake bedrooms, the interiors in which
TV families live out their fake lives. Men with thick
rolls of black tape bouncing on their utility belts
hurry in every direction. Some hang lights behind
reflective screens – tinted ones for outside the
windows, so that with the cameras rolling it'll look
like real sunlight is shining through. A whole world,
constructed piece by piece.

'Who's in charge of all this?' I ask.

'I am,' my dad says.

He's wanted to be a director since he was a little
kid. Now here he is, in Hollywood. Dramas. Always
dramas. I sit in the dark and watch take after take,
sitting in his black canvas chair with cool headphones
clapped over my ears, listening to him give notes.

Let that moment hit you harder. Pause before you deliver that last part about your mother.

He wants more, more. The scene is only working if something bad is happening, the intensity rising to a fever pitch.

Where's the conflict? my dad demands from the shadows. *Locate the conflict.*

Art imitates life, and vice versa. Back in our real house, I find myself rooting for the fights to get worse. I know it isn't the best thing for me, for us, but you have to give the people what they want. Better to be an interesting, miserable family than a boring one.

Let that moment hit you harder, I think, as I listen to them scream through three closed doors and a ceiling, life getting more exciting all the time.

Action, I think. *Action.* ◨

Suppose I Were To Begin

Margaret O'Brien

Suppose I were to begin with the day I cycled over with some food for Dad as he painted the house in Ard Mhuire. He had finished his day's work in the nearby tannery, working with cow hides, and here he was scraping and cleaning walls, and painting them blue to get this terraced house ready for all of us to move into. The cupboard that for years we all referred to as the 'blue press', long after it had been repainted some shade akin to magnolia, must have had its first coat of paint then. We were living in the Connawaries, a couple of miles outside of town, in an old cottage down a winding boreen; and while Dad was painting and cleaning in town Mam was busy at home with her foot-operated Singer sewing machine. She was making curtains, they were blue too, though I may have imagined that detail. But I will say blue because who has any idea of these things now?
On this one remembered occasion I gave Dad his sandwich and he gave me some money. I spent it on a slab of toffee, which was tricky to eat quickly before I got home. I didn't want to have to explain to Mam, to my brothers, that I'd had something that the others hadn't. I was easily confused and shamed it seems to me back then. And it's been a difficult habit to shake. Comes with being female, being the eldest, being the only girl, the only woman after Mam died while we all still lived in that blue house. **H**

Undersigned

Christopher Linforth

Rob, David and I skipped school and hid in the
woods, collecting logs, tossing flaming matches
at one another. The three of us smoked roll-ups,
shouted to each other for a second drag, laughed at
what our teachers had said about our futures. They
had us pegged as academic losers from poor areas
of the city. We pretended not to care that they'd
consigned us to the remedial classes.

David pilfered cans of Stella Artois and strong
cider, and we drank the alcohol behind the
supermarket, saved some for the woods. In the thick
of silver birch and alder, we lit fires and burned
everything we could: books and homework, our
school ties. We listened to Oasis through tinny
speakers and argued over who was the better
brother: joker or singer? We huffed our sweater
sleeves doused in glue thinner and sprayed aerosol
deodorant on our tongues. We danced among the
trees until our legs gave way. Beneath streetlights,
on our way home, Rob scrimshawed our bodies
with biro devils and Celtic crosses and strands of
barbed wire. We bled and we vomited. We resented
our GCSE exams and our school uniforms, the
future wherein we would swapped one blazer and
tie for another. We did not tell our parents any of
this. We were waiting for school to end, for the
teachers to stop talking about career days, about

internships at insurance companies, about sixth-form college en route to university.

These middle-class lives were not for us. We couldn't wait to sign on, get our dole money, spend it at the bookies, the pub. The end of term was close and we were intent on obliterating ourselves. Our nihilism rioted through the woods – every night we could forget about our teachers' proclamations: *stupid, plays truant, unlikely to succeed in life*. We had each other, losers-in-arms; until one of us was gone.

After the funeral Rob and I lose touch. I go on to sixth form, complete the two-year courses without much effort, the impulse to be reckless subsumed beneath David's death. The belt slung around his neck a macabre joke, I heard, a game he was playing with his little brother. Neighbours gossip that Rob took the death hard, assumed it suicide, and spiraled from cocaine to shooting heroin. His parents kicked him out, months after the funeral, the rumors go. Other rumors circulated that I would be next, that I would disappear, one way or another.

But after sixth-form I get a job, try finally to get my life together. Each day, at the social housing corporation, I still cannot conform: I shirk my duties and avoid helping customers with their applications for government benefits. Instead I search for Rob on the Internet. His name so common he becomes impossible to trace, his virtual presence a footnote somewhere inside millions of pages. Before the pubs open, homeless men traipse into the office, up to the counter, where I stand and fake-smile and offer the pretense of helpfulness. Addicts, some of them, ask about local dealers: who to trust and who to avoid? Threats come at me, spat and hollered, pats to pockets and waistbands for secreted knives. One man – my own age – says he will do time for me. A blade in my gullet, in my heart, across my throat. I report him to my boss, who laughs and says the boy was joking. But I know the man is on methadone, that he would erase me and think little of it.

And then I do not see the man for months. I almost forget him, repress his presence in my world like those of Rob and David, until he shuffles into the office, his body thin and blackened with bruises, the hole in his throat swaddled with gauze. He points at me and beckons me over. I stay where I am. He leans over the counter, his blurry eyes trying to fix on my face.

Aren't you going to help me? he says. *Isn't someone here going to help me?* **H**

Collectors

Steve Cushman

We collected guitar picks with bands' names printed on them. This was the early nineties, hair band era and we were young – Todd and Marty and I – in our late teens, and early twenties. Our jobs were not career jobs, but extra-cash jobs, working in a record store, or a pizza parlor, valet parking at a hotel. We hadn't made it to adulthood yet, but we were pulled together because of our ties as guitar pick collectors.

Our favorite bands varied. Mine was Van Halen, Todd's Boston, and Marty loved Kiss, but if Poison or Cinderella rolled into town we would be out there with our pick books, three-inch thick binders with plastic sleeves for storing the picks like precious coins. We showed these to the bands' roadies as proof that we were serious about collecting and wouldn't they like to help us out?

Some did, some didn't. Some picks we had to buy with cash or maybe barter with a nickel bag secured from a friend of a friend. But over a year or two or three – it's hard to believe this only went on for a couple years – we collected thousands of guitar picks. We collected autographs too because we were there and the bands were there, so why not? But it was the picks we were after.

There were girls too, early nineties heavy metal girls with all that hair and those tight skirts. The girls would go off with the roadies onto the tour buses and part of us wanted to go too, even though we knew what they were doing. They would reappear 15-20 minutes later with their shiny laminated backstage pass and we loved them a little, and sometimes a lot, for their part in the rock 'n' roll circus.

Some nights we collected 2 picks, other nights 20-30, and on some glorious nights even as many as 100. We stood in front of the stage and gave that open-handed supplicant pose asking, begging, for a pick as if it were a communion wafer.

The next day we'd meet at Marty's or Todd's house and we'd go over what we'd collected the night before, maybe trade a few – an Eddie Van Halen for a Paul Stanley – and what we wanted, whether we knew it then or not, was to belong, to be part of the greatest show on earth.

Now, as I look through what's left of my pick book, I think of my old friends and I wonder where they are and I miss them more than I probably should because I have a job and a family and a house – hell, a different life. But back then I belonged, we belonged, to each other, to our pick books, to that brotherhood of rock 'n' roll, our hands out, waiting for the slick plastic of a guitar pick, one like we'd never seen before, one that proved we were in this together. ◪

Ekphrasis

*From the Greek ἔκφρασις (ékphrasis), meaning 'description';
a work of art produced as a rhetorical exercise,
in response to another work, real or imagined.*

Helvetia

by Kimmo Rosenthal

'The countries we long for occupy a far larger place in our actual life, at any given moment, than the ordinary country we happen to be in.'
- Marcel Proust, In Search of Lost Time

'Imagination helps us live our lives. We have it because without it we do not have enough.'
- Wallace Stevens, The Necessary Angel

Every one of us, whether we realize it or not, has our own version of Helvetia.

These are the words I wrote after I finished reading the story Emerald Blue for the second time. It would not have occurred to me to write that sentence after my first reading, some two years earlier. At that time I had only thoughts of a young boy looking at his stamp collection and imagining distant landscapes. The strange names on the stamps would evoke images that would continue to appear in his mind in later years, whenever he thought of faraway places where a truer reality might exist; such as the fact that he had become the greatest poet in Helvetia. I remembered as a boy looking at a stamp marked Helvetia and thinking no more than that it must be the native name for Switzerland.

Gerald Murnane's writing has been a touchstone for me and with each reading I discover more. After this latest return to his stories perhaps I am coming closer to understanding how the idea of Helvetia has influenced my own writing and reading. We often travel in our minds to a succession of places. These journeys occur in the absence of time in the interstices between what might be referred to as actual moments. All of these places might be named Helvetia, or they may at times have been our own versions of Romania, as with the narrator of There Were Some Countries, or else a remote island visible from the shore near the Waldo writers' colony in Stone Quarry. In these travels we have been guided by 'the most private of maps' and the thought that 'anything was possible but the actual'.

I can imagine Helvetia as one of Italo Calvino's invisible cities. They all bear the names of women and Helvetia is the female personification of Switzerland, with the country's flag emblazoned on her shield. I think Helvetia would be a 'continuous city', always familiar yet constantly it 'refashions itself', changing with every visit like Calvino's Leonia. No matter how far you may wander, you will remain in Helvetia for one never reaches its boundaries. There are always further outlying regions beyond which lie further never-to-be-explored districts.

If I were to envision Helvetia as a building it would be a secret museum, with an enfilade of rooms stretching endlessly down winding corridors, each room containing paintings hung for private viewings; a place where you can return time and again to encounter these works, some of them utilizing pentimenti – for it has become impossible to reconstruct the original versions, only faint traces remain which become harder to discern with each visit. It seems fitting that the Italian word means repentance. Other paintings are works in progress, changing right before one's eyes in unexpected ways.

Is it possible to describe the true essence of Helvetia? Isn't the nature of Helvetia ultimately beyond our grasp? One can only attempt to list its inherent possibilities, which will differ from person to person.

Helvetia is where a young boy, not yet a man, can dream of the landscapes he has yet to cross and the future selves he imagines he might become, comforted by the consolation of possibility.

Helvetia is where this same boy can approach the freckled young girl with flavescent hair and confide in her what until then had only been words appearing on the imaginary pages he had yet to write.

Helvetia is where the man with the gray at his temples can cast aside the Beckettian refrain 'All of old. Nothing else ever', and abandon the melancholy he feels at having arrived at the wrong destination so many years ago.

Helvetia is where this man, who unlike the younger man no longer dreams, can wistfully look back towards the landscapes he has crossed, hoping to revisit them again as if for the first time.

Helvetia is where, in the words of Proust, one is 'liberated from the contingencies of time', and there is only an eternal present where the intangible can become manifest.

Helvetia is where you might find a private version of Combray with its own Méséglise Way, a place for breathing in ecstasy listening to the rain fall among the lilacs.

Helvetia is where you can explore in the fading shadows of twilight the remotest of solitary landscapes searching for some unknowable meaning.

Helvetia is where a reimagined past comes full circle to meet the imagined future, as in joining the points at infinity on a line to form a circle, yet this circle is without a center.

Helvetia is where you become a character in your own work of fiction, as echoes and remembrances of the past commingle with a new, more palatable narrative created to make the present bearable.

Helvetia is where you might suppose you are living and dreaming at the same time, or where, as Rilke once wrote about dolls, 'you allow yourself to be dreamed.' **H**

This essay was inspired by reading Stream System: The Collected Short Fiction of Gerald Murnane by Gerald Murnane (Farrar, Strauss & Giroux, 2018)

Introducing the winners of the
Hinterland Prize 2019

First place *Anna Lachkaya* for *Sew Me A* Song

Second place *Megan Holland* for *Snake Pass*

Third place *Dani Redd* for *Remembering Ice*

Overleaf, and published in full,
are all three winning pieces.

1st Place

We felt we were in the hands of a writer confident in both their writing ability and their approach to their subject.

– Euan Thorneycroft

Sew me a Song

by Anna Lachkaya

I did not like the brown brick building on the outskirts of downtown Minneapolis, nor the old stalling elevator that took us to the upper floor. The square building looked abandoned in the setting sun. The elevator doors opened, and a single light bulb hung in front of us on a black twisted rope in a gray-walled hallway. We turned to the right and walked through swinging plastic sheets towards the faint hum of sewing machines.

An older woman met us, dressed in black, her demeanor brisk and loud.

'Too small to be fourteen.'

The older girl assured her that the younger one had just turned 14 years old. 'She work hard.'

'She take bus?'

'Brother drop off.'

'Three dollar an hour and no break.' My sister nodded and switched to Latvian.

'This is just for a year until you are fifteen and can start working legally somewhere else. One of us will be back in six hours to pick you up.'

I remembered the vintage European sewing machine of my childhood. It did not compare with the modern tabletop versions lining the tables at this factory. My mother used to sit on a straight-backed chair and work on never-ending dresses for her six daughters. Mother's foot moved the pedal under the table to get the machine tapping loudly, the black metal heavy with swirls of the Singer brand name. The spool pin spun around, thread flowing through the vicious needle with each movement of her foot. My mother talked as she worked, just as she talked when she slept.

The spool pin spun around, thread flowing through the vicious needle with each movement of her foot. My mother talked as she worked, just as she talked when she slept

'Lift the bar by the presser foot, place the fabric on the cloth plate, and lower the presser to trap it...'
'Keep it straight...'
'Keep your fingers away from the needle bar...'

There used to be a *La Modiste* shop within walking distance from my childhood home in Latvia where men and women came to be fitted for a special outfit. It was next to the shoe repair shop, next to the small bakery, at the top of the stairs on the second floor. Once I used the back door and called over the singing sewing machines to ask if there were any scraps of fabric. I had lifted up my small doll. Painted-on underwear was all the doll had, pale naked limbs straight and unmoving. The women working there were nice. They filled my hands with satin, cotton, and silk.

'What is your doll's name?' asked the youngest woman, her dark eyes surrounded by strongly perfumed chestnut hair. I told them.

Atnāc atpakaḷ nākošnedēḷ un mums būs vairāk. 'Come back again next week and we will have more.'

'This... is not a bad place to work,' she said. 'You get a 20-minute lunch if... you work eight hours.'

It was the month of October, our first month in the United States. The snow came early that year, piling up high on the streets and walkways. The factory was chilly. The twenty-some bodies were not warming up the room sufficiently. One night I gave in and used the sharp scissors to cut off the fingers from my knit gloves to keep at least my palms warm. My mother's hand-knit gloves frayed with the cut, deteriorating slowly, coming apart higher and higher on each finger. I kept cutting off the dangling blue threads, afraid the snapping machine would trap my fingers. When the owner walked by and noticed my hands, she reached down, pulled off the gloves and spoke rapidly in a language that I could not understand.

For one whole month, we worked on pillowcases. Rectangular black and orange cases with bats, pumpkins, and scary green monster faces. The fabric felt waxy on my fingers, as if the images had been freshly painted on the cloth. I liked smelling the fabric, the clean scent of the material turned inside out.

The rhythm of the room guided the movement of my hands. Tap-tap-tap, slowly at first, and then faster. Keep within one centimeter of each edge, rotate the fabric, tap, tap, tap, cut the thread, move the pillowcase to the pile and grab two more. Later we all stood at the large tables and turned each pillowcase out, using a metal pointer for the corners. We tied the hanging threads. My arms hurt from lifting them up and moving them down, up and down again. But it was nicer to stand around the tables and move a little, compared to sitting still for hours.

Women and children of different ages surrounded me, rarely talking. Most were Asian, with a handful of white immigrants who could not speak English

Women and children of different ages surrounded me, rarely talking. Most were Asian, with a handful of white immigrants who could not speak English. A thin, angular woman with black hair, possibly of European descent, sat down at one of the tables in the corner and pulled out a square package from her bag. She peeled off the top and slowly made little sandwiches on the table in front of her. Yellow cheese hid a round cracker, and a round salami-looking circle finished the top. The stranger looked up and smiled. Later she came by and introduced herself as Oksana, recently arrived from Ukraine.

Здесъ… не плохо работатъ. Oksana spoke in Russian, a language we both could understand.

'This… is not a bad place to work,' she said. 'You

get a 20-minute lunch if… you work eight hours.'
She spoke fast, as if in a hurry, pausing in the
middle of the sentence to make a point. Sometimes
Oksana saved me a small Lunchables sandwich
and left it on the machine wrapped in tissue. Later
I took it out to the hall on the pretense of using the
restroom. I ate it slowly, taking apart each piece,
stretching the moment.

I loved to help my mother cut the cloth to match the newspaper; and later I would stand like a mannequin as she pinned the pieces on me

As far back as I could remember, my mother used
old newspapers to cut out panels for a clothing
prototype. The different shapes lining the floors
did not make sense at first, until Mother fit them
together like a puzzle. The left chest piece met
with the right chest half in the front. The back was
another portion, and the sleeves yet another. A bell-
shaped skirt was the easiest to make, since it only
needed one seam. I loved to help my mother cut the
cloth to match the newspaper; and later I would
stand like a mannequin as she pinned the pieces
on me, tucking in, drawing the lines with a chalk
that would be taken in even further on the sewing
machine. This system did not work as well on toys. I
only used a needle and a thread to make clothes for
my smallest dolls.

Sometimes I tried to negotiate with my mother.
'I don't want the sleeves so short.'
'Can the skirt go past my knees?'

The answer was always no. The rest of the family needed the fabric.

Payday at the factory was every Friday. The owner placed a small blank envelope on my machine at the end of the day. I counted the money in the restroom, getting to know the foreign currency, the faces of the old men. Most of the time it was $90 even. Sometimes it was less. I did not know how to find the answer for the lesser amounts. Maybe I had used the toilet more often than I should have. When I arrived home late at night, I left the envelope on the kitchen table for my parents. I ate leftovers, poured a cup of strong coffee, and pulled out my schoolbooks and dictionary to start on homework.

The fabrics changed in the winter. They became tougher and heavier, the wool transferring its taste to my mouth, dry and scratchy. My neatness and precise cuts earned me more time at the cutting table. My hands dried, and blisters lined my index finger where the metal scissors dug in. The factory was colder; snow shaded the windows outside, reflecting the lamps and the people indoors. I looked for frost flowers, but curiously, the winter in this country did not grow them.

I noticed that Oksana always seemed to work on the more complicated pieces like coats and jackets. Only she and the owner did not mass-produce the same thing. It was as if these two were the only gifted women in the room, hanging beautiful pieces of clothing on a rack next to their machines. I found excuses to pass by them and touch the buttery soft coats, the velvet pants.

'Someday,' I said to myself.

One time at school, the teacher woke me up, lifting his hand off my shoulder. I struggled out of the seat, grabbing at my books and notebook. Had I blacked out again and fallen asleep? I had moved from the front of the classroom to the back corner just in case this happened. Nothing fell down this time. My feet felt like lead.

'Do you need to talk to anyone?' the teacher asked. He had long silver hair with a black mustache and kind eyes. I could see that he had let me sleep through his whole period and had waited until the other students left the room.

'Nnno. All fine.'

He sent me to the office anyway. The counselor, a talkative woman, went on and on about drinking and partying. At least, I thought that was what the counselor said. Whenever people spoke rapidly in English, I had a hard time understanding all the words. I watched her earnestly and nodded my head any time a question was asked. I took the letter my parents must sign, and folded it neatly before placing it in my backpack. After the meeting, I walked to the school library, picked a corner, sat down and curled over my pack for a few more minutes. The silence lulled; the smell of books comforted. Some days I was so tired I did not care how well I did at school.

Spring finally came. On my way to the factory, I stopped on the side of the road to tear off a few branches of lilacs. I buried my face in the familiar scent, closed my eyes and imagined I was back in Europe, in our backyard. Except these lilacs were dark purple, and mine had been white. I looked at the small blooms carefully, searching for one with five petals instead of the usual four. ◼

2nd Place

Heart-wrenching. Brutally honest with some raw – not flowery – sentences.
– Susan Karen Burton

Snake Pass

by
Megan
Holland

1. The Car

The Snake Pass is a slippery stretch of road that worms through the Peak District and connects Sheffield and Manchester. It's hauntingly beautiful, enveloping cars in plummeting hills and the thickest kind of darkness that you only find in the countryside. Mum and I would travel over it on Friday nights after work, making the pilgrimage back to Sheffield to spend the weekend together.

Mum was a copywriter and I was an account manager, and we worked together at the same advertising agency. It was an unusual arrangement, a constantly shifting relationship as I asked my mum to adhere to deadlines and she reminded me that I needed to get a haircut. If I was coming home for the weekend, I would sneak a lift with her or lounge around after work, drinking several pints of beer before hopping the train and spending the journey trying hard to sober up: swigging bottles of water and racing for some form of fast food. The aim was not to disappoint Mum when I got off the train. I had the independence of a first proper job tangled with the dependence of spending an inordinately high amount of time with my mum. I was fortunate that we had such a good relationship.

The best nights were when we drove over The Snake. We would set off in the light and drive through the dusk, my eyes growing heavy as I entertained daydream after daydream. I'm a travel companion with little energy: I'll sing and chat to you for an hour before fading away into the lull and luxury of the passenger seat.

As a child, I had watched a documentary about a Roman who became lost in the hills and wandered with his torch flickering in the wilderness. A legend had grown around it, that driving late at night you could still see his light as he searched hopelessly for his friends. Even as an adult, it made me shudder whenever I saw a long and lonely light in the hills.

In the quiet, in the dark, the conversation would inevitably come to this:

Are you seeing anyone at the moment?

Not at the moment.

What about Daniel?

Nope.

Jack, John?

Nah. I'm focusing on my career right now.

Don't spend all your energy thinking about work.

I would freeze and my body would grow hot, bubbling with nerves that were red-raw like lava. I would grab hold of my phone and scroll through texts, pretending to engage in conversation with other people. I would try to change the topic. I would switch the radio on and turn it up loud to drown the beating of my heart, the sound of my distress, the beginnings of a panic attack. The Snake no longer safe, the darkness no longer a blanket but a representation of the secret I was withholding from my Mum, and the conversation I was terrified of having. I would tell myself that I was not lying to Mum. I was focusing on my career. But I was seeing someone – and I was gay.

2. The Ice Lolly

Here is everything I remember.

It was the 7th of August, my friend Jess's birthday. At lunchtime, Jess and I had eaten at Yard and Coop and after discovering it was her birthday, they had prepared her a watermelon cocktail for free. Jess drank the cocktail and I ate the watermelon.

My mum had recently started to experience an unusual swelling in her stomach. It made her look as though she was pregnant. She had been to the doctors about it several times and they had dismissed her, telling her that it was the menopause. She was run down and tired. She hadn't been to work in a week and we'd had most of our meetings over Skype. The last time we had spoken, she had looked tired, as though someone had turned her skin grey. The day before, she had messaged to tell me that she'd had a referral to the hospital. I hadn't heard from her since, even though I'd called the night before.

It was the first really hot day of summer after months of substandard weather; the sort of day where nobody gets that much work done because the sun is a huge distraction

It was the first really hot day of summer after months of substandard weather; the sort of day where nobody gets that much work done because the sun is a huge distraction. I sat across from my colleague and we had a competition, in which we played 80s songs and asked our friend to judge who had the best taste. I was winning, even though I wasn't born in the 80s. My colleague was becoming increasingly frustrated as he picked more and more obscure music and I bit back with Time After Time.

I went to see my boss, Olly, and told him that I was worried because I hadn't heard from my mum. I had a niggling feeling in the back of my head that was chipping away at my otherwise perfect summer day. He went out and got a box of ice lollies. I took one. The phone rang. Olly answered it. He handed it to me and told me to take the call in the meeting room.

As Mum was telling me that she had terminal cancer, I observed my ice lolly closely. It was a Rowntree's Fruit Pastille knock off; one of those lollies where you taste an intermittent burst of various flavours that colour your tongue like a rainbow. She told me she had 6 months to a year to live. I started to break the ice lolly into chunks and threw them out of the window, watching them smash on the ground below.

It wasn't possible; was so hard to comprehend that I was speaking to my mum as she told me she was dying: the juxtaposition of being informed about death by the one who has been sentenced. I told her no. I told her I would come home. I ran out of anything else to say, but I felt as though I was burning from the inside out. As though I could have fallen to the floor and smashed into pieces so small that they could never be assembled again.

She told me she had 6 months to a year to live. I started to break the ice lolly into chunks and threw them out of the window, watching them smash on the ground below

I walked out of the room. The office was empty. I told Olly. He drove me home over The Snake. We chatted the whole way, a mediocre conversation that momentarily relieved me from the pain I was feeling inside. There I was, making the journey I made so frequently with Mum, knowing that we might never make it together again.

Later that evening, my girlfriend Emily took the train to Sheffield to join us. She was a nurse and a regular fixture in my life, so it wasn't considered strange that she would be there as a friend. My mum felt safe with her and told her about everything that had happened so far. Sometimes, Mum spoke to Emily in a way that she couldn't speak to the rest of us. Their connection stopped my mum from being so afraid and it made her feel safe. That evening Mum told her that she was part of the family.

I felt guilty. I felt guilty that I was hiding my sexuality. I felt guilty that my sexuality was so prominently on my mind when we were all going through something so awful together. Lots of people came to visit that day and it was overwhelming, so we sat in the background and took photos of my sister's pet rabbits. We didn't really talk to Mum.

3. The Chilli

I wrote a bucket list of things that we would achieve with Mum before she passed away:

A holiday abroad.
Rent a cottage.
A trip to Center Parcs.

I spent a whole day cooking meals in Manchester because I didn't know how else to help. I bought piles of foil takeaway cartons and I cooked vats of chilli, buckets of sausage casserole, beef stew. I separated them into meals for one and meals for two. I laboriously labelled each of them with the contents and the date it was made. I piled them into plastic bags and took them back to Sheffield.

On the train, the contents leaked through until all you could smell was tomato and Worcestershire sauce. My shoulders ached from carrying so much food. When I arrived and presented it to my mum and stepdad, they put it in the freezer. It never got eaten because no one knew what to do with themselves and nobody needed that much food.

That night, I lay in my bed with my sister, Shannon, and we chatted for ages. I turned to her and I took a deep breath and told her that I was gay. She called for our other sister Bethany to come in, and told her. The three of us chatted about it. I was scared. We were raised in a Christian household, where being gay wasn't ever an option. Every time I'd considered coming out in the past, I'd remembered passive homophobic comments, been afraid that the church wouldn't approve of my lifestyle, and was ultimately afraid because I didn't know my family's stance on homosexuality. Were they relaying other people's opinions, or did they genuinely think it was a sin?

My sisters were the first to make me feel safe. They told me they were pleased I wasn't alone. That it was OK. They loved me. They told me that they understood why I wanted to tell Mum and that they would support me through it.

Unexpectedly, much of their reaction stemmed from the fact that they had spent years worried that I was isolated in Manchester. That I had been in love with men but afraid to establish any kind of relationship. They had always assumed that I was some kind of a loner, which was so far from the truth. It was strange to tell them about Emily, who they had known for so long, in a completely different light.

Before they knew we were dating, my sisters hadn't particularly liked Emily. They thought that she was loud and bossy and overprotective. She was all of those things. They didn't know that she was the most selfless person I'd ever known, was kind to a fault; that together we'd started to build a life that was warmth. I told them about how people often

I lay in my bed with my sister, Shannon, and we chatted for ages. I turned to her and I took a deep breath and told her that I was gay

came to visit and fell asleep on our sofa because they felt safe. I told them about how we would have picnics in bed. Go on bar crawls where we challenged ourselves to try different kinds of beer. I told them how we had been together for three years, through the hardship of realising that neither of us was straight. Through the transformative period of leaving university and the gradual steps into adult life. My sisters and I lay in bed and we fell asleep together.

4. The Phone Call

Two years before Mum was diagnosed, she had an operation to remove a tumour on her bowel. The doctors determined that it was not run-of-the-mill bowel cancer, but something significantly rarer. They cut it out and asked if they could study it. We all felt incredibly grateful that it had been caught so early – caught in the midst of another illness and not because it was causing any issues on its own.

It was that strain of rare cancer that Mum was diagnosed with this time around. My dad launched himself into doing as much research as possible to see if there was a cure: looking into programs in America, in Europe – desperate to find out if there was some kind of a way to cure it that hadn't been considered within the NHS. My auntie sent us every kind of vitamin supplement you could imagine and suggested herbal remedies. Every family member had an opinion on how Mum would be able to heal, how we could perhaps increase her lifespan. We read about people who had been diagnosed with terminal cancer and were fortunate enough to live for many years.

A few weeks after her diagnosis, Mum went into hospital to have her stomach drained of fluid. The aim was to remove as much as possible in order to make her comfortable before they agreed on a treatment plan. The drain was not fitted properly and caused Mum considerable pain. The hospital was understaffed and there was little that could be done to ease her discomfort. The drain caused infections. The drain meant that when it came to treatment plans, it felt as though the door was shut on me and my sisters. Conversations were hushed. Nothing was completely clear.

Around the same time, I made the decision to go home to Sheffield and tell Mum that I was gay. I'd decided that I would tell her in person over the weekend. As someone who plans everything in advance, I was filled with extreme trepidation. I became anxious, struggled to speak to her, my mind filled with the knowledge of what I had to do. The cancer made it less scary in some ways. There was no way to get out of telling her. At some point, I would have to spit it out. I was essentially on a timer for the entire thing.

On the way home from work, before I could go back to Sheffield for the weekend, I couldn't take it anymore. I got off the bus three stops early. I grabbed my phone from my pocket. I thought about calling her. I called her. I was walking as quickly as I could, hoping to walk straight out of the emotions I was feeling and into a sense of calm.

I was passing Chorlton Community Church when I told her I was gay. I ran my hand through a bush and tore clumps of leaves from it.

Are you sure?

Yes.

There's a lot going on at the moment, so it might be that you've just developed some intense feelings?

No.

You must have thought I was being ridiculous all the times that I asked if you had a boyfriend. Those times in the car.

I never thought that.

Are you sure?

I'm sure.

I didn't want to put the phone down because I was scared that if I disconnected from her, something terrible would happen. She asked me if she could tell my stepdad. She asked me if she could tell my godmother. I thought about those people knowing. Now that it was out there, it was no longer my secret to keep. For the first time in three years, it would be out of control and it would spread.

Never again would I have such a sense of control over my sense of identity. Revealing yourself, being completely yourself – it's a position of vulnerability.

This wasn't the comfort of a car, rocking me gently over The Snake. This was admitting to the world that I was gay. It was accepting that I was going to carry that openly for the remainder of my life. It was admitting that throughout my mum's cancer, I would need to be open about who I was in order to give the care I needed to give and to be cared for by Emily. It was like taking off my armour and preparing to create a new set from scratch. More of me was exposed, but I would be stronger for it.

5. The Bedroom

Before the cancer, when I went home for the weekend, Mum would sometimes stand outside my bedroom door for ages, mugs of tea clinking in her hands, feet creaking on the landing before asking if she could come in. We would sit side by side on my bed and begin a tenuous conversation that would often trail deeper and deeper until we'd been sat there for hours putting the world to rights, the tea now cold, the rest of our family searching for us within the house.

The first weekend after I told her I was gay, Mum came to my bedroom to talk to me. She was not well enough to make us both a cup of tea. Time was playing tricks with us and, after the issues with the fluid drain, the six months to a year diagnosis was trickling away. The hospital had not told us that it was moving faster but we knew. We knew from the increase in visits from family members. From the trips to A&E in the dead of night. From Emily quietly trying to warn me, having seen similar cases. The cancer was aggressive.

I perched on the bed and Mum leaned against the radiator. She was uncomfortable, always uncomfortable

I perched on the bed and Mum leaned against the radiator. She was uncomfortable, always uncomfortable. She was pale. Later that evening, we would call an ambulance and they would take her to A&E. Over the weekend, unsure of what to do with myself, I would go back and forth in taxis with bags of things that I thought she might need: pillows in every shape and size, books, toiletries. I hoped that one of them would somehow bring her some restoration.

I want to talk to you about what you told me on the phone the other day. I spoke to your Auntie Sue, and she told me that the most important thing is that you feel as though you can be yourself. It must have been difficult to carry that burden.

Her speech was stunted. Partially because of the pain. Partially because of the topic of conversation. We looked at each other and I didn't know what to say or how to explain. There wasn't enough time and there weren't enough words to explain what being gay was. How could I possibly change a lifetime of perception for someone in a short conversation while they were literally dying? I knew that she was searching for a level of understanding. That she had probably had conversations with many people: my coming out another thing to process on top of her own death. That made things complicated. Could it be considered selfish that I had chosen to add to her burden?

> **I knew that she was searching for a level of understanding. That she had probably had conversations with many people: my coming out another thing to process on top of her own death**

There was a knock at the door downstairs and another plethora of people came to visit, to speak to her as though she was a confessional. Perhaps I treated her like a confessional too. She told me that she was in pain. She shifted towards the door. She went downstairs to greet them and we never finished the conversation.

6. The Hospice

Six months to a year became eight weeks. We responded to it by setting a rule: what Mum says, goes. Mum wanted to talk a lot about Judge Judy. She wanted us to turn visitors away. She wanted to eat fish finger sandwiches.

A nurse came over and suggested that she fast track Mum into St Luke's Hospice. She told us we would have to wait for a room to become available and it might not be possible to get one in time. We were fortunate enough that just a day later, one was freed up.

How to explain the respite of a hospice. The beauty of end of life care. Sometimes I speak about the importance of palliative care, the ways that we can guide someone to the end of their life and people don't understand. But at St Luke's we had a beautiful, spacious, comfortable room. We had access to delicious and hearty food. We walked around the grounds. We had massages. St Luke's meant that we didn't have to worry about Mum all the time and that we were looked after too.

Looking after Mum meant being mean sometimes. It meant that people described us as guard dogs and sometimes we had to carry out actions that I didn't want to do. Turning people away who had come to visit. Telling them that they couldn't see her. Ensuring that we weren't gratifying other people but were instead focusing on her and what she needed.

During one of my train journeys, I wrote down everything that I could ever want to say to her in a card. That day, I sat with her and I read it out loud.

I said: Mum, you are my best friend and I don't know what I'll do without you.

When I finished reading, she didn't respond and I wondered if it was too late. If perhaps, my words had never hit home and she would never know what I'd said. Then she turned to me.

She said: That was beautiful.

Mum wrote down everything she wanted to say to me. She was not well enough to read it out loud.

She said: Do not carry the burden of all of this on your own.

After weeks of being afraid that she didn't understand my sexuality, that somehow it had affected our relationship even though we were coming so close to the end, that perhaps she loved me less, I felt safe and content.

7. The Station

I saw Mum leave, life's luggage gathered at her feet.

For days, she had been talking about a train station. About tickets. She wanted me and my sisters to come with her.

The woman who articulated, whose life revolved around words, had ran out of things to say. She tried but they are gone, trapped, finished. I was woken up at five in the morning by a phone call to say that it was time. The night before, my sister and I had left Mum asleep to a channel of meditation music that we didn't know if she could hear. We had discussed whether we should stay, sure that we were coming towards the end.

A panic, a scramble to get hold of all of our relatives who were spread throughout the city – staying with their friends, their family. Worry when Bethany didn't pick up her phone. Clambering into the car and rushing to the hospice hoping that Mum wouldn't let go without us. Let go alone. We gathered around her bed and clung to her. To her skin, her clothes, her hair, scraping and scratching and trying to show don't go, while saying let go. Let go just relax be free let go let go let go. It was animalistic, we crawled across the bed and all the shackles of our emotions that we'd been wearing bravely for Mum fell off.

She was trying desperately hard to hold on. It's the strangest feeling, to tell someone to let go. To tell someone to die. We eased her away from this life and suddenly the spark was out.

Exhausted, Emily and I caught the first train we could back to Manchester. My mum's family clung to each other. My sisters went for a walk. We drifted apart because the thing that was holding us together for those eight weeks was gone. There was no more guilt for being away, no need to come back home.

8. The Car

In another version of the world, Mum and I would be sat in the car, driving over The Snake Pass. I would be going home for the weekend after a recent break-up. Mum would have made me feel better. Would have helped me to articulate the pain I was going through.

Is there anyone else that's caught your eye? Any girls?

Then we would talk about the girls I know. Maybe she would list them.

Maybe I would point out: No Mum, most of them are straight.

Mum probably would have read loads of articles about having a gay daughter. She would have read the Bible. She would have talked to lots of people about it. She would be trying to find a way to accept it and integrate it. It would have been a tumultuous time for us both – but all the same, we'd be there. In the car.

Driving over The Snake to go home. ▮

3rd Place

A unique geographical setting that feels otherworldly and is populated with intriguing characters.

– Freya Dean

Remembering Ice

by Dani Redd

I took the ferry on an afternoon of driving sleet and leaden skies. It was too cold to stand on deck. Instead I watched through the salt-smeared windows as we steered a course past hundreds of low-lying, granite islets. As daylight faded, my focus shifted to the passengers inside the salon: teenagers doing their homework or fiddling with phones; a group of middle-aged men wearing thick fishing jumpers and drinking cups of black coffee. Everyone, except me, on their way home.

The Åland Islands are an archipelago of 6700 small islands, scattered across the Gulf of Bothnia. Their strategic position between Finland and Sweden means they have been colonised by Sweden, ceded to Finland and invaded by Russia. They finally became an autonomous, demilitarised territory of Finland in 1947, maintaining Swedish as their official language. Centuries of occupation have left their marks on the landscape: Bronze Age burial mounds, medieval Swedish castles, a ruined Russian military fortress. Åland is the land in between; a distinct part of both Sweden and Finland, it belongs to neither, but is something else entirely.

The archipelago is divided into concentric zones, or skärgårdar (skär means 'island', while gård refers to a fence), and there is a world of difference between centre and periphery. In the 'Inre Skärgården' – the inner islands – the sea lies quiet in harbours, is channelled into narrow bays and inlets, irrigates fields and forests. But I was heading to Kökar, an island in the 'Yttre Skärgården' (the archipelago's outermost reaches), where water dominates land, where waves wash over ancient granite outcrops.

'It's in Kökar that the true archipelago begins,' they told me in the capital, Mariehamn, on the central island of Fasta Åland. Meanwhile, on Kökar, the islanders referred to Fasta Åland as 'the mainland.'

'You only get to know the real archipelago when you take a boat out among the skerries,' my guide Johanna noted, indicating the tiny granite outcrops lying even further out to sea.

Dreaming of islands is a movement from stability to flux; a dream that carries you ever closer to the water.

My journey from inner to outer islands mirrored the one taken in *Ice*, a novel written by Ulla-Lena Lundberg. It tells the story of a priest and his young family, who move to Kökar in 1946, exchanging the pine forests and glassy waters of the inner archipelago for windswept vistas of ocean and granite. I began reading it on the ferry. As I became immersed in descriptions of sermon writing and winter storms, seal hunts and haymaking, the darkening sky swallowed up the islands outside. I wondered what I would find when the light returned next morning.

I had come to Kökar on a writing residency, desperate to escape the noise of the construction sites reverberating through the walls of my apartment in Bangalore. Those first few days on the island, I barely encountered a soul. Some mornings I woke before sunrise and walked down snow-covered roads, passing stacks of granite and deserted, pastel-coloured summer houses. The only noise was the crunch of my footsteps, and the wind skating the contours of the rock. I watched as the sun rose and my monochromatic surroundings were suddenly ablaze with hues of copper and pink. I stood at the shoreline, where snow edged out past granite and covered the frozen sea, so it was unclear where the land ended and the water began.

Some years, the sea between the islands freezes completely. It's possible to drive from island to island, or even all the way to the mainland. Before they had cars, the islanders would kicksled their way across the frozen ocean.

...*Now that the ice has set, our boundaries have increased a hundredfold, and we've got elbow room and polished floors as far as the eye can see,* Ulla-Lena writes in *Ice.*

The novel demonstrates how much more sociable life becomes during these periods. But the ice becomes fragmentary and treacherous when it melts during spring.

Cycling home after a meeting, the young priest falls into the water and drowns, leaving his family bereft

...When you're sledding bad ice, you have every reason to be careful. Because that's where the currents run, and that's where cracks open up in unexpected places...

It's at this time of year that tragedy strikes. Cycling home after a meeting, the young priest falls into the water and drowns, leaving his family bereft.

I was staying on Kökar during March, the melting season. The thawing snow revealed red granite roads and large, rust-coloured boulders, splotched with lime-green lichen and emerald moss. The white, hallucinatory silhouettes of Arctic hares suddenly became visible. Once the roads were clear, I was able to make use of the residency's bicycle. I struggled against strong gusts of wind to interview bakers, sheep farmers and hotel owners; to explore parts of the island I hadn't reached on foot. I visited the Bronze Age site of Otterböte, where the ground was pockmarked with circular indentations. These were the remains of fire pits made by the island's first settlers, Polish hunters, who used them to melt down the blubber of the seals they caught.

As the temperature rose, the snow transformed to bleak, slanting rain. So I moved my thoughts inside, spending hours reading and writing in a room overlooking the bay. *Ice* was the book that resonated with me most, thanks to its painstaking depiction of the cyclical rhythms of island life, and the sparse beauty of the landscape.

One afternoon, *Ice* came up in a conversation with the residency manager, Johanna.

'You know, you have met a character from that book,' she told me.

Up until this moment, I had assumed that the novel was fictional. But Johanna told me the book was based on Ulla-Lena's family

'When?'

'In the shop, on your second day. Remember I spoke to that woman who runs the museum? That's Sylvia. In the book she's the little girl that looks after the priest's children.'

'Cecilia?'

Johanna nodded.

Up until this moment, I had assumed that the novel was fictional. But Johanna told me the book was based on Ulla-Lena's family. The priest was her father; the novel describes her own birth. *Ice* was a creative reconstruction of an early childhood, and a father, that could no longer be remembered. By Ulla-Lena, at least. It turned out that Sylvia had no such difficulties.

'I'd love to meet her,' I said.

Sylvia was waiting for us on the side of the road; a slender woman with delicate wrinkles and cropped white hair, holding what appeared to be a piece of church pew. She had been fourteen at the time when *Ice* was set. That meant she was now in her eighties, although she didn't look or sound it. She greeted Johanna enthusiastically and handed her the wooden spar.

'What's that?' I asked.

'It's a signpost. Or it will be, when my fiancé carves it for her,' Johanna said, stowing it in the back of the car.

It seemed like people on Kökar were often making things or doing errands for each other. Johanna spent half her time running around after the resident artists; driving them to the shop to buy groceries, picking them up when they got lost on hiking trips. Now she was spending her morning off acting as a translator for my meeting with Sylvia, since I spoke no Swedish.

Johanna got back into the car, and Sylvia climbed into the passenger seat. We carried on driving across the island, past fields of coarse yellow grass and small copses, the stunted trees dwarfed by wide grey skies. The topography of the island has changed since *Ice* was written. In 1946, no trees grew. Any stray shoots were eaten by livestock.

…You have to fight for every blade of grass if your cows and sheep are going to have enough fodder to get them through the winter and spring…

In the days of *Ice*, most islanders were smallholders. But today there are only a couple of farms on the island. As a result, trees have regrown. However unlike the verdant glades of ash, elm and oak on the inner islands (known as lövängar), the trees on Kökar are predominantly birches; their pale trunks resembling outstretched arms, and their thin red branches capillaries.

The passing of the years hasn't just wrought changes to the landscape. On Kökar, the population is aging. Many of the younger inhabitants now grow up and move away, in search of better job opportunities and larger cities. But even so, the island is not as isolated as it once was. A ferry service travels daily to the main island (a ninety-minute journey) while a red granite road links the settlements. It also connects Kökar to the adjacent island of Hamnö (also known as Church Isle, as it's where the church is located). We drove from one island to the other in minutes. But when *Ice* was written, many of the parishioners had to come to church by boat.

Johanna pulled over. Standing beside the car, hair ruffled by gusts of wind, Sylvia began telling me about herself, and how she came to look after the priest's children.

Hers was a story of arrivals and departures, as is the case of many people who grow up on small islands.

'I grew up on Church Isle, but the school was too far to walk from my house. I moved to my aunt's house on another island, Sottunga, where it was closer. But I was lonely without my family, so I was happy to come back to Church Isle and look after the priest's children,' Johanna translated.

In Sweden during the 1940s, school was compulsory until the age of thirteen. Living with the priest and his wife would have been an opportunity for Sylvia to further herself.

   ...It will be a broadening experience for Cecilia, who is clearly intelligent...

On Kökar, the population is aging. Many of the younger inhabitants now grow up and move away, in search of better job opportunities and larger cities

'When I was older, I left the island and trained to become a teacher. I returned thirty years ago, and set up the museum. Now I am helping to re-establish the old route that people on Hamnô took to church, before the main road was built. It's going to be a walking trail for visitors. Would you like to walk it with me?'

'Of course.'

'Have you got any questions for Sylvia?' Johanna asked.

'How much of the book is fiction, and how much is fact?' I asked.

Sylvia began talking animatedly, and Johanna hurried to translate.

'It's a bit of both. The events are real. The priest did die. Lots of my memories are there, like when I took Grunilla (that's Sanna, in the book) to pick wild strawberries while the mother, Maj, was giving birth to Ulla-Lena. But somehow, Ulla-Lena made many of my memories more... spectacular. And there is a lot that was made up. Sometimes people ask me about the minor characters in the book, and which real people they were supposed to represent, but I don't know.'

I wondered how Sylvia must feel to read
a fictionalised account of her past, to see her
memories through someone else's eyes. If I was
charged with writing my own family history, what
would I reconstruct and what would I leave out?
There are already amnesiac gaps in my genealogy.
I know nothing about my maternal grandma,
exiled from her birthplace in Romania when she
was a child. Maybe this is what family history is:
a series of difficult journeys that can no longer be
remembered. I admired Ulla-Lena for rediscovering
hers through someone else's eyes.

We set off on the walk, following the path
taken by the churchgoers seven decades ago, as
it wound through stunted birch woodland. The
route was demarcated by frayed white ribbons tied
to branches. Sylvia explained that she didn't want
the trail to be too clearly marked: 'no signposts,
no apps,' Johanna translated. However, the local
tourism board would be coming out to the island
next week, to discuss publicity for the walk.

Soon, the trail divided in two. The lower route
skirted the headland, offering glimpses of gunmetal-
grey water and a granite shoreline worn smooth
with age. We took the upper route, following Sylvia
slowly upwards across the granite slabs, which were
perilously wet after last night's downpour. Many
people would consider the walking conditions less
than ideal, but Johanna looked down at the stone
with fondness.

'The granite really does look alive today,' she
said, indicating some splotches of luminous green

lichen. 'After it has rained, you can always see the colours so well. In the summer, when it never rains, it looks dead.'

We stopped at the top of the granite slabs, which Sylvia referred to as The Mountain. Spread out below us was a small bay, surrounded by patches of rough grass and sparse copses. According to Sylvia, the bay had a name: Kuttun. She gestured in the opposite direction, inland, where there was a granite crater now covered with trees.

'It means mother's stomach,' Johanna translated. 'All the places on Hamnö are named after body parts'

'Moder-magen.'

'It means mother's stomach,' Johanna translated. 'All the places on Hamnö are named after body parts. Up there is an area known as the intestines. What do you think kuttun means?'

'Mouth?' I guessed.

Sylvia shook her head and said something in Swedish.

'It means 'lady parts',' Johanna translated.

Sylvia smiled impishly when she realised I'd understood.

I re-examined my surroundings. Neither Johanna nor Sylvia knew from where these names had originated, or how old they were. But it was easy to see why the island, rising up from the ocean like a primeval creature, had once been compared to a body.

A little further along the trail, Sylvia stopped to remind me about a scene from *Ice*. There had been a terrible storm one Christmas, and the priest and his wife thought nobody would come to church. But they prepared for worshippers anyway. And much to their surprise, some of the congregation fought their way through the rain.

...*The seas are too high for anyone to want to come by boat in the dark. So they've started early from the villages and now they can be seen in a long row of blinking, swinging lanterns descending the last slope...*

It was Sylvia who had remembered the line of flickering lanterns, the villagers navigating over dark rocks towards the church, and who had described the sight to Ulla-Lena.

Today there was a strong breeze gusting in from the ocean, and we were wrapped up in fleeces and anoraks. It would have been far colder back then,

It was Sylvia who had remembered the line of flickering lanterns, the villagers navigating over dark rocks towards the church

everyone drenched to the skin and the temperature well below freezing.

Upon descending The Mountain, Sylvia stopped next to a large pile of stones, splotched with pale pink lichen, and began to talk. Johanna translated:

'These are stones from the first church on the island. There is a story about how it was built. A ship got wrecked on the island. The islanders were worried that the survivors were pirates. So they killed them all, except one man. It was because he started to sing, and his voice was so beautiful that the islanders became convinced he was a priest or a Franciscan monk. He ended up staying here, and building this church.'

I didn't ask whether the story was true or not. I was beginning to realise that Kökar was an island where fact and fiction, history and myth, were deeply intertwined.

The trees gave way to open spaces. Now the former priest's house and the church were visible. The house was built of wooden planks painted brick red, the traditional colour of houses on Åland. The smooth metal roof was a more modern addition. Sylvia grimaced at it.

'Ulla-Lena does not like that roof.'

Beyond the house was the 'new' church, constructed in 1784, although parts of it had been torn down and rebuilt since then. It was perched close to the edge of the island. Red pigment from the roof had dripped onto the rough white walls. They were stained the same shade of pink as the lichen on the ruins of the older church.

Before we looked around either house or church, Sylvia led us to a small outhouse. She opened the door, revealing a glimpse of rusty coils of wire and some power tools, and embarked on a long story, translated by Johanna.

'This was the priest's shed. Downstairs was the storehouse, where hams and other food were kept. After the priest died, they put the body in here. I was told to go into the outhouse and get food, but refused, because the shed was dark and I was scared. Sister Hanna, who was helping, told me, "Don't be silly. It's only Pehr in there, and he's not scary. It's not the people who are dead you need to worry about – it's the ones who are alive you need to watch out for." So, I went into the shed; and after, I was no longer scared of the dark.'

Sister Hanna's words of warning reminded me of another scene in *Ice*. Then, as now, many people visited the islands over summer. The island's only hotel opens its doors, summer houses are aired out, and the deserted marina suddenly fills with boats.

…It's no exaggeration to call it an invasion. They come like outright raiding parties…

Ice details an occasion where Sylvia had to sleep in the sauna after a sudden influx of summer guests. While she was sleeping, an 'amorous visitor' burst into the sauna. Sylvia freed herself and hurried to the priest's house in tears.

… 'He said I was sweet,' she sobs. 'He wanted a kiss.' She shudders and cries…

I hadn't brought the incident up, for fear of embarrassing or upsetting Sylvia. But as we passed the old sauna, she mentioned it herself.

'It did happen. But it was a group of soldiers who came. They were stroking my legs, and I ran up to the house because I was scared. The priest's wife got as angry in real life as in the book. But she and Pehr never slept in the sauna.'

I couldn't tell if the memory had upset Sylvia. But I got the impression that whatever her emotional connection to the incident, she was interested in how it had been rewritten and reframed for the novel.

Later, when we visited the museum, I would discover that Sylvia was also a writer; she'd published several books about the history, culture and myths of Kökar. To her, like Ulla-Lena, the island was saturated with stories.

Sylvia pointed out a dilapidated barn.

'That's where Maj used to go and cry after the priest died.'

We walked past without looking inside. Stories belong to the people who lived them, and sometimes it feels disrespectful to delve too deeply

In *Ice*, Maj finds it difficult to express her grief in public. It's only when alone, milking the cows in the secrecy of the barn, that she gives way to her sorrow.

…Yes, there by the cows, she's crying, wiping her eyes and her nose on the sleeve of her milking coat, starts milking again, stops, shakes and sobs…

We walked past without looking inside. Stories belong to the people who lived them, and sometimes it feels disrespectful to delve too deeply.

Sylvia unlocked the front door. We stepped inside the priest's house. It was far larger than I expected, with spacious, light-filled rooms panelled in pale wood. Sylvia took us upstairs to a small attic bedroom.

'This was the first time I ever had a room of my own. The priest's wife put flowers on the dresser. That was the first time someone picked flowers for me too. It made me so happy.'

Standing in the middle of the room, Sylvia smiled at the memory.

'Who lives here now?' I asked.

'They are going to use these attic bedrooms for visitors. Soon some Franciscan monks are coming to stay.'

Downstairs, in the kitchen, the original wood-stove sat alongside an electric hob and a dishwasher. Sylvia wandered through the downstairs reception rooms, talking rapidly, while Johanna followed, struggling to translate some of the memories that were flooding back.

'That space by the window is where I sat with Ulla-Lena when she was little, telling her stories. I loved to tell stories…'

'…Everyone had a place at the table, but after the priest's death, his wife moved places, so she could see his grave through the window. She never spoke to anyone about the death, but she started to look very old, with wrinkles around the eyes…'

Sylvia continued to reminisce, informing us through Johanna that Ulla-Lena had depicted her mother and father with great accuracy in the novel

Sylvia continued to reminisce, informing us through Johanna that Ulla-Lena had depicted her mother and father with great accuracy in the novel.

'But one thing she didn't mention was that Maj hated compliments. I would sing for the guests who came to visit. And whenever anyone complimented me, Maj would say, "but there are lots of other little girls who can sing well too." She didn't like people to feel that they were more special than anyone else…'

… 'After he died, the priest became almost like a saint. Everyone really loved the family. Almost all the families on the island kept a picture of the priest and his family – many still have it…'

The rooms of the empty house were rapidly

filling with memories.

Eventually, Sylvia fell silent. She asked if I had any questions. I wanted to know what had happened after the story had ended, as anyone who reads a good book does.

'What happened to the family?' I asked.

'They were allowed to stay for a year. Then they left for another island, and finally the mainland, where the priest's wife got a job. But they had a summer house on Kökar, and would come back every summer.'

Sylvia travelled rapidly through the decades, telling us about other books Ulla-Lena had written. She told us that Ulla-Lena's mother never remarried. That her sister, Grunilla, developed a muscle-wasting illness and ended up in a wheelchair. This did not appear to have deterred her sense of adventure. Ulla-Lena had gone with her sister on a trip around the world to explore cave art from different cultures, which they were both fascinated by. But although Ulla-Lena had travelled widely, she always returned to the island. The place where you are born always tugs at you, even after you stop perceiving it as home.

In *Ice*, according to one of the older characters, the dead still dwell among the living, watching and guiding.

…The whole world was full of signs. They told you when you should run for home before the storm caught you. They showed you where the fish were…

It felt to Sylvia as if the dead were very much

alive; that events that had unfolded years ago were as clear as if they had occurred yesterday.

The graveyard lay next to the church. Beyond it, the granite sloped down to slate-coloured seas. Sylvia showed us the grave where Ulla-Lena's parents were buried; marked with a granite slab that must have been hewn from the island itself. 'Pehr Lundberg' and 'Maj Lundberg' had been etched into the stone. Even these two names told a poignant story. The priest's name was fainter, eroded by six decades of storms, while Maj's name looked newly carved, making it obvious how much time they had been apart. Grunilla's gravestone was just behind. It was a slab of polished red and black marble, her name inscribed in gold. Just like their characters in the book, they had become text: names that people read, stories people told.

I looked over at Sylvia. She did not appear solemn or upset. In fact, she had left the churchyard and was making her way over the rocks beyond. She sang loudly into the wind as she jumped

Just like their characters in the book, they had become text: names that people read, stories people told

precariously from boulder to boulder. Johanna looked at me in alarm and we followed after her. Minutes later, Sylvia stopped and pointed out a geometric pattern engraved into the rock.

'It's a compass rose,' Johanna explained. 'Sail to the right, and you'll reach Finland. Sail to the left and it's open seas all the way to Gotland.'

Looking out at the slate grey ocean and the bare rocky islets breaking its surface, I didn't feel as if we were close to land at all. It felt like we were standing on the edge of everything. But after meeting Sylvia, I knew that this stark world of granite and ice was far less empty than it appeared to be. The stony outcrop I stood upon was inscribed with layers of memories. As I thought about everything Sylvia had told me, I realised that *Ice* had overspilled its pages. For the first time in my life, I had read beyond the end of the book. ▯

Author's note: All quotations have been taken from the English edition of Ulla-Lena Lundberg's *Ice*, published by Sort of Books in 2016

The Hinterland Prize 2019
Announcing our short and longlists

We were privileged to have had so many fantastic pieces of non-fiction entered into The Hinterland Prize 2019. It made forming a longlist very difficult and narrowing that down a still harder task.

Huge congratulations to all our listed entries – all were sterling pieces of work and their inclusion here is richly deserved.

Winners:
1st - Anna Lachkaya
2nd - Megan Holland
3rd - Dani Redd

Shortlist:
Alison Baxter
Garnett Cohen
Sally Fox
Sarah Hymas
Shauna Jones

Longlist:
Rahad Abir
Lawrence Brazier
Lauren Brown
Savannah Carlin
Kinga Cybulska
Jay Drinkall
Peter Fong
Cathrin Hagey
Kim Hare
Polis Loizou
Claire Lynch
Laura-Blaise McDowell
Jess Morgan
Toby Norways

Yeoyu —
new voices
Korea

Han Kang
Bae Suah
Han Yujoo
Kim Soom
Kang Hwagil
Jeon Sungtae
Cheon Heerahn
Hwang Jungeun

The
Crooked

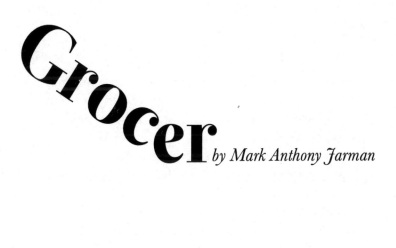

Grocer

by Mark Anthony Jarman

*There was variety of opinions amongst us about the
embalmed person.*
> — A Journal of the Pilgrims at Plymouth, 1622

Good and bad coin cannot circulate together.
> — Sir Thomas Gresham (1519-1579),
> letter to Queen Elizabeth I

Wake up, silent brother, wake up, my dead one.
Has your eye seen a river held mirror-smooth by
a weir? The water impeded pauses and rises in a
curved lens; lifts, then pulses softly over the weir's
moss-green lip.

Will I ever forget that Scandinavian woman
reaping wheat on a rocky hillside in Norway, one
stalk at a time with a small scythe, a blonde woman
up in the clouds with a blade and kernels of grain.
We fill our hands. Haunted by sun on her white
ribbed blouse as she hikes uphill, Nordic light on
her familiar breasts and long hair. Liv is American,
Iowan, but each summer she visits Norway to live on
a misty mountain tilted over deep fjords, seawater
in the land's cleavage, part of the family of hill-
siders worrying a crop in the Scandinavian rocks.

Another side of Liv's family hails from forests in black Prussia, their women run over by too many armies and horses, cousins made crazy by a night's flashing rockets and sister Golden Hair's nightmare fear of rape in the cellars. Now the armies and rubble cellars are gone, now there are fat geese, now Volvos with halogen headlights illuminate their coastal road and Liv drinks tea and reads Dante with her aunts, surrounded by peaks, icebergs and crazy scarlet roosters.

High in Norway Liv works reaping summer's crop and on the farm she eats, she grows, putting on weight. Liv is not pregnant; at her uncle's mountain farm she works hard and brings a healthy appetite to a table of plates and steaming pots, smoked fish, butter and bread and a vivid wheel of nippy cheese.

Liv returns to Iowa City at the end of her overseas summer and I return from Canada. I love Liv, her peaceful presence, yet when I see her again that fall in Iowa City I fear this visible change. Her appetite and my fear. Young and stupid, I fear that future *her*, hips growing, breasts spilling out of her white bra. Liv looks beautiful and I am uneasy.

In Iowa City Patrick is caretaking the house on Lower Muscatine Road where his brother died of a cocaine overdose. I never met Patrick's brother. I pay a very low $50 a month for a room in the dead brother's house; I suspect Patrick is happy for the company. I traveled to Iowa City with little but a backpack, but the house has it all: stereo and stacks of vinyl, glasses, plates, popcorn and salsa; pots and pans in the kitchen, an iron woodstove and a daily *Des Moines Register* (a fabulous newspaper then); the weekend Chicago and New York papers and the UK's *New Music Express*, our kitchen stacked high with papers.

Patrick, a former journalist, grew up near here on the Mississippi River in a town famous for a Heinz ketchup plant looming over Mark Twain's house, roads decorated with tomatoes fallen from farm-trucks.

Patrick found his silent brother in the living room and Patrick threw objects at the still body, a mug, a book, whatever was handy, yelling *Wake up, wake up*, knowing the truth, yet not wanting to believe.

... a town famous for a Heinz ketchup plant looming over Mark Twain's house, roads decorated with tomatoes fallen from farm-trucks

The city crept toward this sagging farmhouse and kept going around it. A Hardee's franchise directly across the street from our door where we can jog over for hot breakfast biscuits and beside it a Baptist church sign that I study as if for an exam: *It was not nails that held him; it was love.*

Patrick is a native son happy to show me around his state in a beaten Mazda, a car once green, but now bleached by summers and winters to no color.. In September we were both nervous rookies at the Iowa Writers' Workshop. I spoke to Patrick at The Mill tavern minutes before I was to sign a lease at The Rebel Motel, an address that seemed *tres* cool a-là Tom Waits living at the Tropicana Motel. Patrick's house is better.

So all of us actors travel to this rainy door in the USA. A knock and Liv stands at my screen door, Pat's door, her brother's black pickup truck visible in the driveway, the driveway where I toss dead mice from the kitchen traps all winter to freeze solid on the tarmac. Liv at my door just a moment, she is leaving soon in her brother's truck, arriving and leaving, that hovering moment in the portal where life can go either way.

We've been apart for a few weeks, Liv's face near mine, her sweet face wet with rain; we kiss, we have tender feelings for each other. I touch Liv's face, push back blonde hair from her face and we kiss again, rain dripping in the doorway, rain general on Iowa's endless corn and red-winged blackbirds. I open her cowboy shirt and with some vague hope Liv lets me hold her in my hands, lets me weigh her wares like a crooked grocer.

Liv is good, it hurts my heart that she allows me to look at her again, her risk with other people so close, her shy offering at the door where Liv looks in my eyes and wonders, she must try, the beautiful moment where Liv lets me look once more and I let myself look at her round flesh though I'm pretty sure our future has no future. I am a bad coin circulating. Liv climbs summer mountains, her parents church-going Lutherans who eat church-hall lutefisk under the old rugged cross and send eyeglasses to Africa. They do the right thing.

Who am I to judge Liv or reject Liv? Downtown the police read blood in a parking lot. 'He tried to get away.' She grows, she grows grain while I grow nothing.

I don't know which way to look, which way to move, my thumb on the scale and I don't want to choose, don't want this power, this roll of tumbling dice.

Do we *always* feel we are with the wrong person? Upstairs sleeps a woman from California who rides horses and will marry me and come to regret her choice. I find the California woman witty, but she is also headstrong, turbulent, a poet of the slow burn, the long held grudge. Liv is kind and peaceful, down to earth, so predictable. Liv doesn't cry at the door, Liv the calmest person in the world. That calm attractive in hindsight, but back then I was trying to live in a punk record, I was seeking chaos. How to understand that the green whim and hope of a few seconds can steer the rest of your decades, your piece of a century.

Wake up, silent brother, wake up, my dead one. I am alive and Patrick's brother's heart stopped by an opiate, your life decided by thimbles and whim. How often I adore the moment, but not the moment directly after, or the moment two decades later. Distant futures wait for you like a mirage on the highway, a body on a highway. Why is it so much easier for me to recognize my past cruelty, yet not read today's lapses in charity and clarity?

At the door in the rain I hold Liv tight as we kiss each other, kiss goodbye. What words can there be at such a door? Liv had laryngitis when we first met, a husky voice, a mouth full of honey. Meetings are wonderful. Versus not meeting. Every few days, in unfashionable yellow plaid bellbottoms, Liv walks to work at Montgomery Ward, *Monkey Ward*,

she calls it, an anchor store in the disagreeable
downtown mall that ate rows of charming shops
and cockroaches, stolid brick walls suddenly fragile
and tipping over, walls blurred in a crusade of
urban renewal.

Her lost voice low, *hello*, Liv whispered to me
at the party in Iowa, her hand low on me at the
Hawkeye game in Nebraska, in the Eden Motel in
South Dakota, Liv steering a truck as golden light
touches the crops and a funnel cloud appears to us
resembling a solid Roman pillar. She was my best
opiate. How can you map this foreign landscape,
accurately test a lost moment like an airport swab?
This embalmed era defeats me, wears me down like
cocaine stopped the brother's heart as Neil Young
sang in his ear, *Well hello Mr. Soul.*

Cocaine, prime bud, and sheets of acid; one hundred hits thin as ancient parchment and you need so little

Cocaine, prime bud, and sheets of acid; one
hundred hits thin as ancient parchment and you
need so little. Windowpane and purple dragon
grown under lights, wax hash oil, heroin and meth.
Iowa City is drug city, not what I expected in corn-
fed Iowa. Weigh it out, man, Crockett a tennis shoe
hustler in army pants and a Marley t-shirt moving
quarters and eight balls and fat white bags of crank
sealed with grey duct tape. Product moves from
Houston to Chicago, so logically some of it alights
in Iowa City plunked beside Interstate-80.

'Not much product around,' says Crockett, but

players and hustlers always bemoan this shortage. He irons his money to remove the wrinkles from the addicts' tight pockets and hands; irons to make the bills seem cleaner and it looks so domestic. Did Crockett kill Patrick's brother? *Someone* killed him. At first we thought coke was safe, *nose candy*. Then not. Then the ODs and depression and shakedowns and shakes and seizures, collapsed veins and bored detectives in a van watching a jittery target and people not sleeping and other people not waking up and families learn of cardiac arrhythmia.

'Now I personally don't use drugs,' says Crockett, but his customers are going at it hammer and tong. 'Sativa is nice,' he says, 'you can focus.'

Liv likes to eat and Heather our favorite undergrad writer eats diet pills and worries about her weight. A weird thing: word of an OD gets around and Crockett's sales go up. Bad PR is good PR to an addict. There it is. It's money; Crockett is putting himself through law school and ironing dollar bills to clean them; we contain contradictions, we go ask Alice, but no one learns any lessons. Just one more taste, corral some more wrinkled cash and save the planet later; we'll do it tomorrow. First thing!

Monstrous feelings of iron regret the next calendar day. OK, this time let's *really* change our life, charity work in Haiti, a ski bum high in the Andes, or live among the Esquimaux under a northern sky shifting to shadow, burn bridges and seek a new purity on a vast plain of ice storing its own white hues in a world turning bluer and bluer. But escape is never pure.

Blonde grain in the steep rocks and Liv's scythe
goes dull nicking against stone: sharpen the blade,
cut stalks, sharpen the blade again, iron teeth
rasping a mountain in Norway. The sun never sets
and Liv works her Scandinavian summer, midnight
light hung over the mountain; Liv loves meals in
a farm kitchen, buttery home cooking her opiate.
Iowa is where I saw my first personal computer
and where I first saw Americans of real girth,
jovial citizens devouring heaps of syrupy hotcakes
and steaks and biscuits in chicken gravy, Middle
America mailing cash to Tricky Dick and Teflon
Reagan while ingesting a million ballpark dogs
washed down with Blatz beer. America, America,
I am guilty of being superficial, but such a giant
neighbor makes one nervous.

Patrick's place, our place, was a bit of a party house.
Now that I am older and bourgeois I wonder if
neighbors watched through curtains, if they hated
us. We cared not a whit for the noise and weedy yard
full of golf carts. Our purple sofa caught fire one
night from a bohemian candle and soon we owned
blazing curtains! A panicky miracle, we put out the
fires with a bucket of mop water and dragged the
sofa outside to smoke blackly atop a snowbank.
    Sans sofa we play vinyl in the living room where
his brother died, spin Eno and Fripp, Wire, Talking
Heads, Magazine, Laurie Anderson, Los Lobos,
X, Gun Club. But the dance crowd wants catchy
Motown hits, not new wave or no wave or shoegazer
or punk. They complain to Patrick of stepping on

frozen mice like rocks in our driveway and they complain of my depresso Joy Division records; they dislike *Dead Souls*, *Atrocity Exhibition*, *Isolation*, *Shadowplay*, they want to twist the night away and shake some action.

Before he died Patrick's dead brother was renovating his aged house; the main floor boasts table-saws and planers and some walls are open rows of 2x4s; we stroll past power tools and exposed studs and dancers pogo around circular saw blades. At one party Patrick's file cabinets slide open from vibrations and pounding, from music and dancers, and the weight in the long metal drawers makes the towers begin to topple; dancers strain to hold them up and call to us for help.

The entire house shakes as dancers jump up and down and bend the hardwood, which has an awful lot of give, but is it strong enough?

The entire house shakes as dancers jump up and down and bend the hardwood, which has an awful lot of give, but is it strong enough? I descend stairs into a basement cluttered with the brother's head-shop paraphernalia to gaze up at wood wowing above me, curious to see if the floor opens. It holds, the bough does not break, dancers dance on and mice hide in the hollows and wait.

Every night Patrick makes popcorn laden with butter and salt, our ritual, and he introduces me to scalding peppers and salsa and spicy platters of Mexican food from the many Mexican families who settled in Iowa for truck farming and work at the smelly ketchup plant and started very good Mexican restaurants in scattered small towns. Patrick, who loves Mexican food and Heileman's Cream Ale, is not slim. Patrick threw pots at his slimmer brother dead of cocaine, threw panicked pots and books and yelled in sorrow, *Wake up, wake up!*

Patrick's dead brother left behind a strange Zundapp motorcycle and a green Porsche 914 2.0, a hot mid-engine two-seater with removable roof and pop-up headlights, and this sports car rusts in our mice-littered driveway, the boxy Porsche locked in litigation that dooms the car.

After Patrick found his brother's body a stranger appeared. 'Hey, your brother sold me that green Porsche before he died. There was a *deal*, the Porsche is *my* car.'

I'm afraid not, said the grieving family. A lawsuit, and winter and summer a valuable sports car rusts in our driveway, engineered beauty beached on flat tires.

Patrick sings and plays guitar in a country-bluegrass-folk band, his new girlfriend from Wisconsin on vocals and banjo. Liv and I tag along one sunny afternoon, drive the bleached Mazda into the country to a biker bar on a pretty green river shaded by trees and running with farm pesticides. The band sings and plays from chairs, no stage, and we drink booze from clunky mason jars and I understand the Elvis line, *drink my liquor from an old jam jar.* Giant black letters **FTW** in a stark message on the white ceiling.

In this bar by a green river we watch big men force a bent safety pin through the pale meat of a young man's bloody ear lobe, a service, the initiate giddy with pain and joy, so happy in red blood because now the biker colors can be patched on his leather vest.

Patrick sings some good obscure covers, One Meatball, Do-Re-Mi, Green on Red. This country bar, their *church*, runs out of kegs, runs out of bottles, runs dry of all beer. No problem; the bartender drives lickety-split to a store and walks back in from Iowa sunlight with boxes of canned beer they sell to us straight out of the boxes. You would not see this in Canada, but it keeps the party going in the land of the free.

The letters FTW on the ceiling. What's FTW?

Fuck the world.

Ah. FTW!

Liv laughs and wheels on an Iowa dance floor in black lace and denim, she is warm, living and palpable. Who am I to turn on her, to place all on an uncertain dice roll? Everyone likes her, wants to dance with her, but she is not conceited and she loves me and on a Norwegian hillside she cuts summer grain while I grow nothing. Am I dead in feelings, am I fleet of foot, are my curtains on fire?

In winter our old house is frigid, though I feed scrounged wood into the potbelly stove. Patrick wakes one night to find a mouse curled fast asleep in the tiny bowl of his solar plexus, his mouse seeking warm sanctuary. Patrick lets the creature stay warm, Pat such a gentle soul. Liv is also gentle.

Both native Iowans are far kinder than me. Pat keeps the heat low fearing a future lawsuit from his five-year old nephew who technically owns the house. Welcome to the paranoid world of the USA where you wait decades to be sued by the assessing eye of your dead brother's child.

Welcome to the paranoid world of the USA where you wait decades to be sued by the assessing eye of your dead brother's child

Liv drives to this door, *come back to me*, say her pale eyes, her pale lids, *give me a chance.* He loves her, she loves him, then maybe he loves her not. Liv fills my hands with a banana loaf wrapped neatly in foil. *Eat Me!* says her note. I read the note and my guilty stomach hurts. She baked it herself in her mother's kitchen. Her mother likes me. Liv and I used to cycle in the country past Iowa's monstrous hogs with huge dinosaur maws and Liv told me stories of farmers on the ground, say a heart attack, and the farmer's loyal dog saving the farmer from those jaws eating him down in the muck.

When cycling out in the cornfields the rattling noise of stalks and stiff leaves is surprisingly spooky, and then a tap-dancer noise – tiny hooves of piglets crossing the hard road in front of us – this is also a real surprise, stiff-legged piglets fast and nimble as kittens before they turn fat and old. Crazy red-winged blackbirds dive-bomb our bare heads wanting hair for their nests in the marsh. Eat me, says Liv's note. I devour her and Liv tastes of lutefisk and corn, pork and beans.

Squirrels poke their heads out of holes inside the house's unfinished walls and their tense glossy eyes stare at me as if to check: *did we miss a budget meeting?* One day I am on the commode and a mother squirrel looks out and then introduces her baby squirrels, as if to say, *This is the Canadian guy who lives here.*

Enough, I say. I prop open the front door and chase the little dervishes with a pellet pistol I found in the house. Strangely, herding squirrels out the open door works (versus herding cats), but then I'm a ludicrous sight on an American street, in the driveway wearing boxers and wielding a pistol. Or maybe I'm perfect for the corner of Church and State.

I'm a ludicrous sight on an American street, in the driveway wearing boxers and wielding a pistol. Or maybe I'm perfect for the corner of Church and State

An elderly man ambles past with a walking stick on his way to Walgreens and cheerfully says, 'I'm slow as a turtle, but man, I'll get there.'

I'll never be slow as a turtle, never be old; a messiah with so many lives, I'll never OD. These are my locust years, the years the locust hath eaten. In Iowa City I want everything and it all seems possible. Didn't I know yet that straddling two or three worlds never works? I didn't know that yet, though Patrick pointed it out to me, many people tried to point it out.

At the Shamrock Tavern the California poet, mad at something I said, stomped out of the bar. A pattern of her being mad at me.

Don't follow her, said Patrick. Just let her go.

I followed the woman from California, caught up on the street and we made up, made a life, had beautiful children. What if I had not followed her? Looking back, I wonder now if Pat preferred Liv, wonder if Pat was trying to influence me. A new thought, but I can't ask Patrick, it's too late.

Patrick's father was a traveling salesman and also worked in the brother's head shop, a middle-aged man in suit and tie selling pipes and psychedelic posters and waterbeds and small coke mirrors, Willy Loman prowling a head shop. The basement full of such tiny mirrors. Pat's father bought 38 golf carts at rock-bottom price to flip them at a profit, never quite got round to the crucial flipping stage and 38 golf carts sit for years behind the house, weeds climbing over wheels and axles, rusting like the Porsche rusts.

During Iowa's long winter I discover a Porsche key in a drawer. Now the Porsche is my car. I study the car and I think about the car more than anyone else, therefore it is mine. My simple plan: come sunny spring I will drive the Porsche all the way to the Canadian border. I have no legal papers, but I will not draw attention to myself, I will calm my blood in a stolen car and keep the Porsche near the speed limit through the Dakota badlands, then I will park the car in northern Montana as close to Canada as possible, not wanting to risk the car at the border. On long roads I will speed into the Bitter Root range and Glacier National Park, and maybe some sunny spring-skiing, go skiing in a life moving at the speed of light, the speed of wheels on a dead man's Porsche. I know my way to the distant peaks.

I stole a car on the west coast a few years before this. Walking and broke, I sensed a key, some kind of thievery ESP. I sat in the car, pulled down the visor, and *ping*, a key fell to the floor. I wanted the whole world and it seemed to be there.

But that dog ain't gonna hunt for long. The Porsche is lifeless, refuses to turn over and we remain paralyzed on flat tires, my dead speedster won't climb a Montana mountain to see that wet bear climb from the river with a salmon and shake itself dry, its whole body moving in parts. The costly German car rusts away like a shopping cart and no one makes it eat the corners, not me, not the covetous stranger, not the grieving family, not the lawyer with his beautiful shirts.

FTW, mutters the dead brother in my ear; the dead brother wanted his fast car to hit the road once more.

Instead of my mountains, did the Porsche 914 travel to a hinterland scrapyard out by the mothballed meatpacking plant? And I wonder if Liv still travels to her mountain in Norway, flies an ocean to cut summer grain above her Viking fjords.

The last address I remember for Liv was Colorado, where she taught kindergarten. Patrick followed me to Seattle and I saw him a lot. I worked illegally mowing lawns and clearing brush. Pat blossomed in Seattle, playing in bands, writing ad copy, writing speeches for the Governor, even getting a grant from The Grateful Dead to fund a local zine. He was the unofficial mayor of Belltown back when Belltown was a risky neighborhood in the monorail shadow. This was pre-grunge. What was that good bar with stunning huevos rancheros – the Two Bells?

We moved to Canada, approaching the border with no paperwork (try doing that now), drove her Datsun across the border and then went east

At Seattle City Hall I married the California poet; and we moved to Canada, approaching the border with no paperwork (try doing that now), drove her Datsun across the border and then went east and slowly lost touch with Pat. And now the email: Patrick is dead. One morning in Seattle he simply does not wake up, another brother, another heart stopped before its time as the light fails and turns blue on his Fremont street.

Seattle, Iowa, New Brunswick, Norway: they're basically the same assortment of brothers and sisters, voices and cellars, salt and potatoes, rivers and skies, good coin and bad coin. Our ancestors sailed with their few coins and died in tents the first winter. No grain wavering on the hillside. They got there too early; no, they arrived too late, a clerical error. Longboat Vikings row up the river one pleasant summer to see if the new mall is open yet.

Liv's Lutheran church stands aloof in infinite fields of corn just past the Rebel Motel. Liv's long blonde hair in the sun, Liv folding sweaters downtown. Her blond brothers stoned and dangerous, yet she is good as custard. Anything I did was OK with her. Liv's drugged blond brothers 86ed from every bar in Iowa City, yet she never once raised her voice. We never argued, but I wanted out. Can you be dulled out by kindness, by goodness?

Liv said to me, *Are you not even going to try?* One of Liv's brothers was thought dead of an overdose, but rose again to walk among us asking for more poison. Did Liv's outlaw brothers know Patrick's brother? Were they party to that fatal OD?

That very last visit Liv drives away in her brother's souped-up black truck, her back turned to me, something in her eyes. Downtown a young man locked in the cop shop because of a commodity, an exchange. Now he's praying and retching while police watch him on CCTV and laugh. *He's toast.* He married the wrong brand.

There is something comforting about eating at the sink: it catches your crumbs, forgives your sins

I do not fly to Patrick's funeral, do not send a message. There is something comforting about eating at the sink: it catches your crumbs, forgives your sins. Hostile lightning writes something on the horizon and I fill a saucer of water and this water reflects a bird motoring past: a bird flies outside my kitchen window and its twin image flies across my saucer of water. How complicated is domestic life and the dead offices of adulthood. So many perfectly aligned lines of light travel 93 million miles so a swift bird bisects a trembling lens of water and my eye ready to receive.

Something in Liv's eyes was once for me, she was happy growing things in our earth, her back bent over the sunny garden, yellow gourds rising in warm soil like bright loaves. Liv rides a stallion in white forests draped in lichen beards, Liv rides a quaint train station to station, climbs her mountain in sublime dusk, soft blues and whites with a violet tinge, a scary lovely landscape, a fjord pale as her skin, but sky going dark as the black glow around a burning candle. Liv's long golden hair flew about her body and all wanted to dance with her.

And I have learned to love the hall that empties, preferring the quiet. A river valley's beautiful cold blue draining of light in sombre degrees, a covered bridge darker and darker – just another evening in the world, yet seeming loaded as a pistol, portentous.

On a hill above town white smoke billows from an industrial chimney, smoke billows into blue sky and flattens in freezing wind and winter sun bright behind it, high white smoke back-lit, pure white clouds edged with gold; a beautiful vista for a few moments and I expect angels to float over the water.

Times I may want to kill myself, but I also love these many lives we have, love the lives we had and states we visit briefly, flying years of candles and birthday sighs and false messiahs, fanatic screams of glee and grief, a lifetime of a family's gifts to each other, good coin and bad coin.

Times I want some electric change, to skate up a river to Hudson's Bay, skate in herds of wolves and white bears running sad ice; I want the option of vanishing in a pair of binoculars, to vanish into the cataract tracts of a true north, my summer gone like freckled whales.

Times I give up on life – it's clearly over, clearly done like dinner – but then I am allowed to unhook a dress, voilà, a back stripped so bare that it's a shock, an open new country, a heart pumping altered pagan blood and I am born for this fierce thrill. What I am here for? Am I not here for this?

A friend has a brain aneurysm and she is lucky to not veer into oncoming headlights. Patrick's brother dead of a whim. And I am still alive, like Liv's lucky brother who rose from death to life in a new country, by moving water, a grassy path by the canal and a distant figure past the weir. The people waiting seem to know us, the green landscape vaguely familiar. These strange dreams; perhaps they coach us for dementia, to visit her bare white back in the garden and travel in trees darkening by a covered bridge. The ruffian on the stairs with a knife, the figure by the pointillist canal. Can I pass by?

Patrick's basement has boxes of small coke mirrors, minor basement narratives. I can't forget that family on a northern farm; one by one they descend rough steps into a root cellar dug out beneath the farmhouse.

The father says, *What's keeping your sister?*

I don't know. I'll go look.

There is no air or bad air in the root cellar and each human falls to a packed floor dug in our earth, sister, brother, father, all losing each other, one after the other descending into a vegetable earth that dimly takes us.

Somewhere in a lit living world a woman I
once loved reaches for a lamp, and someone else –
mechanic, teacher, doctor, tattooed house painter –
someone else studies her hand near a lamp, notes the
rope intricacies of her hair's stiff braid in the pleasant
yellow light of her reading lamp, her jolly corner.

She was good and I hope she is happy in her
corner and I hope she has forgotten that rainy day
at my door. I was not a perfect person, I wanted
out, wanted the chaos of several lives, wanted to
drive all 38 golf carts out of our ruined yard all at
the same time. I left and left again and I am happy
in my life now where rain is gentle and a river cold
and generous. In Iowa City the bus stops by the
tracks and I climb aboard. I know the driver, a big
man from Mississippi who played football with the
Hawkeyes a year before they made it to the Rose
Bowl in California. All children become immigrants;
exiled in woods with a wounded horse to cross a
glowing river with grief's bone caught in our throat
like exalted birdsong. Mirror-smooth water pulses
softly over the weir's mossy lip and down into a canal
bisecting green fields and hedgerows and a yellow
hotel as in a blurred oil painting where a veiled figure
awaits your return to a perfect world.

But you can't go back and you can't have it both
ways. Either your curtains are on fire or they are not
on fire, you follow her when she leaves The Shamrock
or you don't follow. There is no in-between. **H**

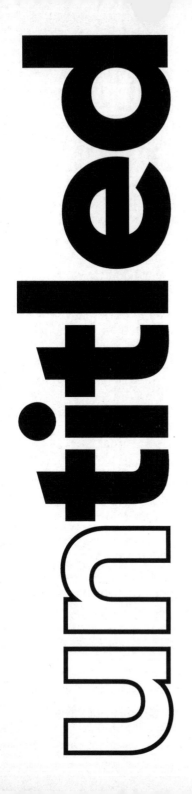

You thought you knew the whole story...

Come and celebrate with us at Untitled writers' events - a new platform for underrepresented writers to share their work in front of an audience. There are no limitations to what might be shared and we know there'll be something for everyone.

To find out more about Untitled, let us know if you want to share your work in the future and to find news about our next event in October visit **untitledwriting.co.uk**

🐦 writinguntitled 　📷 untitled_writing

Festivals & events
Online writing courses
Face-to-face workshops
Weekly writing life podcast
Free writing resources

Sign-up to our newsletter for regular updates:

nationalcentreforwriting.org.uk

Follow  WritersCentre

 National Centre
for Writing

Key funders

   ARTS COUNCIL ENGLAND

 NORWICH City Council

 UEA University of East Anglia

How
To
Do
The
Job

by Bella Braxton

2.46 pm

Look at your store. Wrap your arms around
it. Unfurl yourself from that fetal posture of
ambivalence. Let your body be enough for you.
Walk into your store.

3.04 pm

Pack the bags, sweep the floors, push the carts. Wonder how much eye contact is necessary. Decide on little to none. Put the meat in a separate bag. Be careful with the eggs and make sure that the people see that you are being careful with their eggs. Wrap the glass in paper when necessary. Listen to exaggerated grunts when you put too much in one bag.

Be aware that they are watching you, but not so aware that you are afraid to move. Be aware, also, that you still belong to yourself, and that no amount of looking will make you theirs.

Keep your own eyes on the apples, the cans and the plastic bags. If you see babies or small children with their parents, you may want to look at them. Do not look at them. If you do, everyone will think you are a pedophile.

3.26 pm

Sweep the onion peels into the dustpan. When someone asks you a question stare blankly at them for at least five seconds.

When someone asks you if you speak English nod slowly. The slowness of your nod may be interpreted as uncertainty. Crack your knuckles one by one. They will ask again, louder this time. Say yes.

Sweep up even the small things. Even the things that appear too small to matter, because many small things accumulate to make big things.

3.47 pm

Tell the person it's OK; no, they don't have to pay for it. Pick up pieces of broken glass with your hands. Listen to your own blood scream excitement. Let it remind you of your mortality.

Resist the urge to run to those you work with, saying, *Look! I also suffer!*

Let your fingers stick together. Pull them apart. Wipe the blood on the inside of your pocket.

Mop up the wine. Let the wine soak through the holes in your shoes and into your socks. Let it enter your bloodstream through the semipermeable membrane of your skin. Stand in your own dizziness.

4.02 pm

Push the broom across the floor. Go fast. Don't bump into him. Whisper *excuse me*. Whisper *sorry*. Go slow. Find yourself unable to decide between breathing through your nose or mouth. If the onion peels float away, pick up the broom and set it on top of them. Hold them down.

Shake the broom up and down, breathe in the dust, blink it out of your eyes. Feel whole. If the dustpan is not where it should be, look first in the refrigerated room filled with broccoli, grapes and okra.

If you happen to have swept up any coins, pick up the coins and put them on the shelf where you have lined up the many other coins you have accumulated. Suppress the urge to dance.

4.09 pm

Enter the break room. Stand in front of the time clock trying to remember whether you just did a store sweep or a produce sweep. A store sweep. Press the button. If someone else is in the break room you might want to talk to them.

Let yourself talk to them. Try to make them laugh. Say whatever makes them smile. Be willing to die for anyone who takes the time to look at you.

Think about what they say. Wonder what it could possibly mean. Adopt their personality traits as your own.

4.19 pm

Use the trash can to prop open the bathroom door. Smell the stomach acid. Know human nature inside out.

Put the paper towels, the small trash bag and the multipurpose cleaning spray on the fold-down baby changing table. Lean the handle of the mop against the wall. Wear gloves. Turn your head away from the vomit to pull in gasps of clean air.

5.05 pm

Walk across two parking lots to bring back the shopping cart full of trash. Let yourself be angry. At whoever left this cart here, at the air for being too cold and at your parents for forcing you into such a vulnerable existence.

Be angry at the people you work with for not telling you the things they tell each other. Be angry at yourself for not being the type of person they would want to tell those things.

Notice that there is no one around. Suppress the urge to run out of the shopping complex and to never stop running. Push stacks of carts into your beautiful store.

Learn how to get the exact right amount of carts into each entrance. There are two entrances. Most people will enter through the right side and leave through the left.

If a man is walking towards the entrance fast and has no children, he will take a basket or nothing at all. Women with small children or babies take big carts. Old people and young women without children or with older children take small carts.

6.24 pm

Clock out for your lunch break. Sit down in the chair closest to the door, facing the lockers. Breathe.

Do not eat during your break. Do not drink. Don't look at your phone. Fold your hands in your lap and think.

It is possible that many of your co-workers will be in the room as well. Say nothing; live off what falls on the floor as they eat.

It is also possible that one of your favorite co-workers will be there too. Maybe their break is the same time as yours. Possibly you will be alone with them. In this case, you will want to talk to them.

If they are not looking at their phone, or otherwise engaged in another activity, you may talk to them. Try to say something interesting. If they don't look interested, stop talking. They don't want to talk to you. After this point, any attempt to initiate conversation will make them hate you.

If your co-worker does seem interested in conversing with you, do not become overexcited. Don't monopolize the conversation. Especially, don't interrupt them. Let them know that you experience emotion too. Let them know that you are human.

Don't stare at your co-worker. They might become afraid that you will rape them. Try to look slightly to the left or right instead of looking directly at them. Do not breathe heavily. Hunch your shoulders forward in order to appear smaller and less threatening.

Do not remember everything your co-worker says to you. If you do, never let them know that you remember. That would come across as creepy. If you are ever asked, or prompted in any way to recall details of a conversation, make strained faces and gaze into the air above your head as you 'try to remember'.

Do not say anything that in any way conflicts with the way that you think they see you. If you say anything contradictory to your 'personality' (the version of yourself that you have presented to them) they will think that you have been lying to them about who you are.

Do not laugh unless they are laughing. If you do, they will think there is something wrong with you. Don't use words they might not know. This will make them feel bad and then they will hate you. Do not make jokes unless you have a contingency plan, which, in the case that they do not find your joke funny, would allow you to pretend that what you said was never meant to be funny in the first place.

If you find that you really do need to look directly at your co-worker, look only at their face. Never look at any other part of their body, especially not their breasts or anything else that could be misconstrued as some sort of sexual predation.

When your co-worker leaves, you might feel like they hate you. You might feel like crying, but never cry. If they forgot something in the break room and come back in, they will see you crying and it will make them feel uncomfortable and they will hate you forever.

Instead of crying, think about everything you could have said but didn't while your co-worker was still in the break room with you. Think about how stupid everything you said was. Think about what your co-worker said. Wonder what it could possibly mean.

Think about how pretty she is. Don't think about how pretty she is, it's bad. Don't think.

6.50 pm

Push the broom between the registers and, if your co-worker looks at you, you can look back at her. Smile, for the attempt at its reciprocation: allow yourself this one last sin. Swallow her smile whole. You will be hungry for a friend: a sister or mother.

Know that nothing will ever be as wonderful as it could be. Pull the burden of that knowledge to your chin like a blanket, and rest assured that it will always be there.

Consider the possibility that she only pretended to smile at you – or, perhaps, she never smiled at all and you only wanted her to so badly that you believed that she did in fact smile, as a mirage of water might appear in the desert. Maybe she was smiling, but not smiling at you. Maybe she was smiling at someone behind you, at such an angle that made it seem as if the smile was directed towards you when it wasn't.

Maybe your own smile was not enough to oblige a response. Consider this. Maybe even your whitest teeth are yellowed by malnourishment, maybe your hair is not shiny but dull. Maybe your body is shriveled, curling inward and she has mistaken you for a rodent.

Blink the dust from your eyes. Maybe she is afraid. Sweep up the dust.

7.03 pm

You may see the sun beginning to set. Do not be afraid. It will rise again tomorrow.

7.19 pm

If there is trash in the trash can already, dump it into the compactor. It might be heavy; bend your knees and push up past everything like a flower growing in the sidewalk. If it is heavier than heavy, push harder. Think, one more time. If it is still too heavy, give up. Hang your dull, yellowed head.

Push your shriveled hands into the trash can. Pull out fistfuls of corn husks and throw them into the compactor's gaping mouth. Pull out whole apples and cartons of rotted strawberries.

Work quickly. The clock is moving. Pretend not to care.

Push the large trash can to each small trash can. After transferring the contents of the small can's trash bag into the large can, return the bag to its original can to avoid wastefulness.

When you get to the registers, the cashiers will be standing directly in front of the tiny trash cans at each of their respective registers. You will need them to move. Staring blankly toward your co-workers will sometimes result in the required movement. Be patient. Do not breathe heavily. Direct your eyes toward the ceiling or floor.

Ache with a feverish warmth.

If the manager's office is locked you will need

to find someone with the key to unlock it for you, usually a manager. Search until you find them; be aware of the clock's subtle movement.

Eventually, your body will begin to work independently of your mind. Allow this change to occur. Use your idle mind to think of her.

She may be leaving soon. Watch for her to slide the 'checkout closed' sign to the end of her register. This moment is vital.

Contrive some way for you to be near the door when she walks out. Take care to appear engaged in some other task. Look up, slightly to her left or right. She will wave at you. Do not lift your own hand in return.

Smile, but do not bare your teeth.

7.54 pm

The mop bucket will probably be filled with brown water. It will smell like fish. Dump it out and fill it with the floor cleaning solution. Watch white bubbles replace brown sewage.

Push the mop bucket as quickly as you can out of the back room. Lean the wooden handle of the mop against the coat hangers on the right of the door to the men's restroom.

Walk to the registers as quickly as you can. Limp if you must, but limp quickly. Tear the plastic off of a new roll of paper towels. Choose a bottle of multi-purpose cleaning spray.

8.06 pm

If a customer tries to enter the restrooms while you are cleaning, you have to let them in. Pace outside the door hugging your paper towel roll to your chest.

Maybe her smile was only a reflex and had no meaning. Maybe she always forgets your name but you never notice her eyes drifting down to your name tag.

8.40 pm

Push the carts. The atoms are moving slowly and your fingers will turn red and white. Know that soon you will find warmth.

9.48 pm

Push the vacuum cleaner back and forth. Keep watching her, if she is still there. She might leave early. Maybe late. When she leaves she will not think of you until you see her again.

Do not deceive yourself, as you are a deluded creature already.

10.05 pm

Clock out and walk in her vague direction.
Say goodbye if you want. Don't think of her.
    Love your store as you walk out of its beautiful doors. Into the cold night.
    Save your wondering for later, and it all will be resolved the next time she looks at you. Cave under the weight of her laughter as the door closes behind you.
    And again, tomorrow. ▪

SONS OF NEPTUNE

by Andrew Menard

For many years now I have walked out of my plain brick apartment building, turned to the left, and followed the long, rigidly parsed streets of lower Manhattan to a promenade that overlooks the East River.

The East River is really an estuary – a river that runs both ways – rising and falling with the ocean tides, adding the astringent smell of salt water to the mechanized, oil-fired urban air. Cantankerous seagulls stand facing into the wind on its decrepit pilings. Predatory cormorants terrorize its murky depths. Flat-eyed flounder from Long Island Sound flutter below hungry blue fish streaming in from the continental shelf. When the river is glassy and slack, pausing for a moment before reversing course, the world seems to lose its bearings.

I often stand beside the river like one of the pensive ocean dreamers in *Moby Dick's* opening pages – drawn to the 'extremist limit of the land' because it reminds me that Manhattan is an island. To the south is Liberty Island and Ellis Island and the busy waters of New York Harbor. Still farther south is the narrow mouth of the harbor and the wind-swept finger of land known as Sandy Hook Point. However, I am lured by even deeper waters – by the pelagic blue abyss that lies *beyond* Sandy Hook Point. For it is there, where the continental shelf drops away, the water seems heavier than before, and the horizon becomes a firmer line of yearning and excitement, that so much of my early life was shaped.

One of the great truths of my early life is that my father was generally lost to me. Leading one expedition after another to the Pacific Ocean, he was not simply gone for several months at a time, but gone to places that could not be located on any map or globe, at least not within several hundred miles and sometimes much farther. Even placing my finger on the spot where he might be, I could never be sure where he was. Maybe he had been there before, maybe he would be there soon, maybe he would never be there at all. No wonder the maps that meant the most to me were almost entirely a featureless blue. Rather than bringing me closer to my father, the indifferent latitudes and longitudes of these empty areas invariably set me adrift, left me stranded in a way that may have had something to do with why I found as much solace as adventure in books like *Treasure Island* and *Robinson Crusoe*.

I've seen Wes Anderson's *The Life Aquatic with Steve Zissou* several times since it came out in 2004. Though I'm not sure why, watching the character that Owen Wilson plays – a man who believes a famous oceanographer is his missing father – takes some of the sting out of my early years. Maybe it's because the mournful and quixotic movie, in particular the scene where the 'jaguar shark' swims into view, is so lovingly dedicated to Jacques Cousteau – already an important figure in Anderson's *Rushmore*, and the antithesis of Bill Murray's gloomy Zissou character.

When I was fourteen, I met Cousteau. My father was on sabbatical that year, and after he finished surveying a profile of the ocean bottom from Martinique to Gibraltar, the rest of the family met his ship in Monaco. As the small, top-heavy vessel, bristling with winches and dredges and various other scientific equipment, churned sideways into its berth, Cousteau bounded down the length of the unsteady dock and stood swaying and waving beside us. I don't recall if he was wearing the red bonnet that was such a familiar part of his public image, but I can still picture the deep lines in his face, rippling like a sequence of waves from his mouth to his eyes.

For some reason Cousteau loved American peanut butter. Knowing this, my father had had the foresight to pack a case of Skippy's along with the rest of his gear. When he eventually handed the peanut butter over – in a kind of parody of the formal gift exchanges that were so common among early expeditions to the South Pacific – Cousteau showed why he occasionally liked to call himself an 'impresario of scientists' rather than a scientist per se. Instead of just accepting the gift and politely putting it aside, he immediately ripped a hole in the cardboard box, grabbed the nearest jar, twisted the top off, plunged a forefinger into the creamy mass, levered out a huge dollop, examined it a moment, then stuck it in his mouth and stood there chewing with a pleased expression on his face. It was such a typical and charming gesture that I assume he was as pleased with himself as the peanut butter. Afterward, he invited us to lunch at the new Oceanographic Institute.

With a French flair for the erotic, he had gradually made both the aqua lung and scuba diving sexy, featuring it in all his books and movies

While we were at the Institute, Cousteau showed us a prototype of the aqua lung he and a colleague had invented in the early 1940s. With a French flair for the erotic, he had gradually made both the aqua lung and scuba diving sexy, featuring it in all his books and movies, an inseparable part of the colorful and romantic undersea world he helped to popularize. But when I learned to dive myself a few years later, my instructor was missing a large, very unsexy chunk of flesh from his right forearm, taken by an aggressive shark off a remote South Pacific reef. The man was a real-life version of the pink-finned, fictional diver eaten by the jaguar shark in *The Life Aquatic*. And I have never entered the water since without thinking of his mangled, half-bitten arm.

That same summer my father took me to see Jacques Piccard's laboratory in Lausanne. Several years before, Piccard had braved the full weight of the Pacific by taking the bathyscaphe he'd invented to its deepest point – the Mariana Trench – nearly seven miles down. After decades of hearing about the Himalayas and the Hindu Kush, people were suddenly aware the Earth had a bottom as well as a top. Of course, it wasn't the 'hard bottom, rocks in place' that Henry David Thoreau made so much of in *Walden*. Instead, it was the unstable, tumultuous morphology of 'hot spots' and 'subduction zones'; a sphere in which a set of enormous tectonic plates endlessly collided and crumpled and dove beneath one another to become ductile again.

Like Cousteau, Piccard was mainly an engineer; walking into his laboratory was like walking into a dazzling mechanical maze. But as he showed us around, moving from one thing to the next with a tall, reserved intensity that matched Cousteau's exuberance, I had a hard time following what he said. I knew the pieces of half-assembled components had been milled to some sort of specification, that they conformed to some sort of blueprint and were about to be assembled into some sort of model. I knew they embodied a precise and accurate vision of an apparatus that would work. But I couldn't see the connections, couldn't make out the shape of the thing to come. Nor could I make the leap from this nuts-and-bolts world to his more romantic and adventurous dive.

Sadly, Piccard's historic dive has always seemed more like a feat – like swimming the English Channel or soloing the Atlantic Ocean – than the kind of endeavour that led Cousteau to become one of the leading environmentalists of his day. Certainly that's how the dive came across in an ad campaign for Hennessy's Wild Rabbit that ran in 2016. The campaign included both a standalone ad and a commentary on how the ad was made, narrated by the rapper Nas. Not surprisingly, the ad was the more dramatic of the two. After showing two men – one struggling against the deafening effects of wind pressure, high in the sky; the other struggling against the silent threat of water pressure, deep under water – the stirring visuals gave way to plain white type on a black background. First: 'In 1931, Auguste Piccard became the first man to reach the stratosphere.' Then: 'In 1960, his son Jacques became the first man to reach the ocean's deepest point.' Followed by: 'What's Your White Rabbit?' and 'Never stop. Never settle.'

Clearly the ad was all staged wonder and special effects – *engineered* effects – altogether different from the visionary practicalities that had made Piccard's historic dive possible. On the other hand, it had been many years since the alchemy of age had changed my romanticism from a dull gold to a rich lead. And armed as I was now with what Marcel Duchamp called an 'indifferent' eye, I found that even as the ad trivialized Piccard's most celebrated and sublime moment, my own bewildering experience began to seem more poetic. As a matter of fact, the ad actually made me feel closer to the experience than at any time since the visit itself. *Ars longa, vita brevis.*

When Charles Darwin crossed the equator for the first time – at a point many days south of my father's transatlantic route – he had nothing good to say about the event. Indeed, he found it close to unbearable. A journal entry, written the next day, reads like an early account of water-boarding:

> 17th *We have crossed the Equator, & I have undergone the disagreeable operation of being shaved. About 9 o'clock this morning we poor "griffins", two & thirty in number, were put altogether on the lower deck. —The hatchways were battened down, so we were in the dark & very hot. —Presently four of Neptunes constables came to us, & one by one led us up on deck. —I was the first & escaped easily: I nevertheless found this watery ordeal sufficiently disagreeable. —Before coming up, the constable blindfolded me & thus lead along, buckets of water were thundered all around; I was then placed on a plank, which could be easily tilted up into a large bath of water. —They then lathered my face & mouth with pitch and paint, & scraped some of it off with a piece of roughened iron hoop. —a signal being given I was tilted head over heels into the water, where two men received me & ducked me. —at last, glad enough, I escaped.*

Fortunately, that wasn't what happened to me when I crossed the equator more than a century later. I was sixteen at the time, working as a kitchen helper on a ship where my father was chief scientist. We had left our berth in San Diego in early summer and would eventually steam hundreds of miles farther south to an area west of Chile. There we began zigzagging back and forth like the line on an Etch-a-Sketch pad as scientists and graduate students plotted the Pacific bottom, measured its heat flow, trailed a magnetometer scratched by the teeth of passing sharks, and occasionally stopped to lower a sediment core or dredge for rocks.

> **all we had to do was run a gauntlet of half-inebriated scientists and crew members – many dressed like women, with mops for wigs and coconut shells for breasts**

Though I was easily the youngest person on board, I was not the only one about to 'cross the line' for the first time. Most of the graduate students had never been to sea before, and one or two crew members had never been this far south. None of us knew what to expect.

It turned out that we were simply the butt of an elaborate, well-choreographed joke. True, our hair was chopped off and we were locked in a dark section of the hold for a while, just like Darwin and his fellow 'griffins.' But that's as far as the two ceremonies overlapped. When the hatch door was abruptly wrenched opened and we were herded up a steep ladder onto the glaring hot deck, all we had to do was run a gauntlet of half-inebriated scientists and crew members – many dressed like women, with mops for wigs and coconut shells for breasts

– none of whom had malice in their eyes or hit us with anything more harmful than a wet sponge.

Once we reached the end of the gauntlet, each of us was pushed to our knees and laughingly compelled to kiss the Royal Baby's ass – really the belly of the cook – darkly smeared with axle grease. Holding a make-shift version of Neptune's trident in one hand, the cook used his other hand to pull us as far as he could into his warm, yielding flesh, rubbing our faces back and forth in a good-natured, if suffocating, way.

Thus were we all initiated into 'the mysteries of the Deep.' Thus we were all reborn as 'Sons of Neptune.' Of course the ceremony was antiquated and silly, and almost laughably blind to its homoeroticism. But the repressed did not return in a rage. There was none of the cruelty Darwin encountered, nor anything life-threatening or hazardous. In fact, within the closely regulated society of the ship – where fears of disturbing a fine-tuned comity were so strong that when one of the crew members cut off half his mustache to see how people would react, almost no one noticed – the crossing ceremony felt like a joyful celebration of the human body. For the most part, we chose to ignore our vulnerability on the ship. But because we depended on each other for our lives – as scientists and sailors always do, even on a modern research vessel – it felt good to rejoice in what Walt Whitman once called the 'ordinary cheer and magnetism' that allowed us to work as one under even the most dangerous and extraordinary conditions. For a few hours, at least, we sang the body aquatic.

One of my favorite works by the group known as Art & Language is a linotype entitled *Map of a Thirty-Six Square Mile Surface Area of the Pacific Ocean West of Oahu*. The work is just a blank white square, outlined by a thin black line, on a blank sheet of white paper. The scale is indicated: '3 inches: 1 mile.' As is the latitude of the southern side and the longitude of the western side, though neither was written large enough for me to make them out in the book where I saw the work reproduced years ago, and they aren't any clearer on the websites where the work can be seen now. This seems fitting somehow; it reminds me of the years I failed to locate my father on a map.

On the other hand, it also reminds me of how extraordinary it feels to experience that kind of blankness firsthand. Standing on the deck of a tiny ship, surrounded by the earth's largest body of water, is almost unspeakably sublime. There aren't many places on the surface of the globe where we can so tangibly front its limitlessness face to face. In a certain light, when the sea is a dead calm and the sky a uniform gray, even the encircling horizon seems to vanish—not drop away or steadily retreat, the way it does on a Rocky Mountain peak or in the vastness of the Great Plains. It's as if you're suspended midway between heaven and earth, your imagination waxing weightless in wonder, with only the acrid smell of diesel to remind you that your feet are still anchored to the steel deck. If there's a better example of how our inability to estimate the size and extent of the world we inhabit can awaken a transcendental faculty in us – as Immanuel Kant famously claimed – I haven't found it. Steaming south from Tahiti to Valparaiso, Chile, you eventually reach a spot where you're farther from land than anyplace else on earth.

Just as crossing the equator reverses both the annual seasons and the direction hurricanes spin, so does the sublime occasionally give way to a gushing, adrenaline-spiked fear of actual physical harm. When Pip, the cabin boy in *Moby Dick*, is washed overboard during a whale hunt, he is rescued by 'the merest chance' and the fright, 'the intense concentration of self in the middle of such a heartless immensity,' is so severe that he is never himself again. In the era of wind-driven ships, falling overboard or sinking were considered such hopeless predicaments that sailors rarely learned to swim, figuring it was better to die quickly.

Since my father wasn't much of a swimmer either, he was lucky that on the day an undersea camera came unlashed, slid across the heaving deck, and cracked him in the head and spine, a crew member was close enough to grab him before he went over the side. When the cook came to tell me what had happened, I swept aside the pile of potatoes I was peeling and rushed to the infirmary.

Time became a sequence of flash bulbs popping in the darkness, stark as a Weegee photograph, but in color: my father sitting hunched and awkward on a grey metal stool; the nearly matching color of his cheeks hollowed out with pain; the bright red blood streaming down his head and shoulders; the doctor standing behind him trying to staunch the blood with a huge wad of white gauze, while other glistening wads formed a deep red clump around his feet. As the fragmented images burned their way into my brain, the bottom of my stomach dropped away and I had to lean over to keep from fainting.

> **As the fragmented images burned their way into my brain, the bottom of my stomach dropped away and I had to lean over to keep from fainting**

My father must have caught this movement out of the corner of his eye, because he turned his head, saw the look on my face, and calmly remarked, 'It's just a scalp wound. They usually look worse than they are.' Though the words themselves didn't register until a minute or two later, both his composure and the way his instinct for rational explanation kicked in made me think he would be OK.

Certainly he was right about the scalp wound: a few stitches, a thick bandage and that was it. But the contusions in his lower back – all black-and-blue from the weight and speed of the camera striking him – were a different matter. Though he acted like nothing was wrong, the way he sat or stood made it clear that his back was getting worse by the day. Finally, the pain became so severe that the doctor radioed ahead to make sure there would be a plane to San Diego on the day we docked in Valparaiso. X-rays taken in San

Diego showed that the camera's impact had fractured, and partially fused, three vertebrae.

Just after turning nineteen, I joined a second expedition; this time as a low-level lab assistant. I boarded the ship in Suva, Fiji, and except for a few hours on the island of Tongatapu, spent the next month and a half monitoring the same scratchy, black-and-white bottom profiles that came to mind when I chanced upon the Art & Language map years later.

Mostly, we crisscrossed the northern half of the Tonga Trench, surveying the second deepest spot on earth. Steaming east from Tongatapu, I felt a kind of aesthetic jolt as I watched the bottom drop away on the echo sounder – the thick, plotted line growing steeper and jumpier by the minute – until it finally flattened out more than 30,000 feet down and then shoaled again just as steeply. Surveys like this had already lent weight to the theory of plate tectonics and soon it would become clear that the Earth basically recycles itself by expanding along a single Mid-Atlantic Rise – steadily widening the gap between the continents east and west of it, while subsiding along a series of trenches that rim the gigantic Pacific Plate. Scientists still wonder when this global carapace first formed. But they've found that it's subsiding most quickly in the depths of the Tonga Trench.

The night we docked in Pago Pago, American Samoa, I met a strangely beseeching girl. She looked a year or two younger than me, and contrary to most Pacific Islanders her hair wasn't long, loose and straight but chopped very short and curled. As we came abreast of one another on the dock – my sense of balance still a little off while I adjusted to a world that wasn't moving underneath me anymore – she asked if I wanted to go back to the ship with her. Since it was the late sixties, and my head teemed with Margaret Mead's *Coming of Age in Samoa*, I still believed there was something called 'free love' – and that it must be even freer and more natural here than in Haight-Ashbury, the East Village, or a commune in New Mexico. Walking one behind the other up the gangway, I noticed a couple of the crew smirking at us. Later I learned she'd had sex with both of them before she ran into me – which may explain why she stared straight ahead as we passed them. But she wasn't really interested in sex with any of us. For as we lay supple and sweaty afterwards, pressed close together in my narrow bunk, she abruptly wrapped her arms around me, pulled me tight, told me her name was Cookie, and asked if I would go home with her.

Why she picked me, I'll never know. Nor am I sure why I agreed. I can't imagine my curiosity was so confounded that I lost track of what I might be getting myself into. But several hours later I found myself on the other side of the island, lying next to her on a woven mat, surrounded by mosquito netting and the shapes and sounds of people fast asleep in an open-sided *fale*. Feeling very vulnerable all of a sudden I kept reaching for her and she kept pushing me away. Eventually, I just lay flat on my back, staring into the darkness above, wondering how her family would react when they woke up. Somewhere a radio was playing – and in a moment of almost hallucinatory cultural slippage, I heard Marvin Gaye and Tammi Terrell singing *Ain't No Mountain High Enough*.

Surprise: no one paid me any attention in the morning. Maybe they nodded, but mainly they just dressed and left. Even when Cookie dragged me outside to meet her grandmother, the woman barely glanced in my direction – not unfriendly, but as if my being there reminded her of something she preferred not to see. For a moment or two, she actually stared into space. But the sadness and contempt that settled in her eyes once Cookie began to weave me into a story of moving to the United States – a story her grandmother had clearly heard in one form or another before – told me all I needed to know about why I was there. I couldn't understand everything they said – much of it was in Samoan – but Cookie's gestures had a parallel anguish and I got the gist.

in a moment of almost hallucinatory cultural slippage, I heard Marvin Gaye and Tammi Terrell singing *Ain't No Mountain High Enough*

I felt completely paralyzed by such a raw, self-destructive display of yearning. How do you comfort someone who seeks her most fervent dream in the arms of boys like me? How do you comfort someone whose shorn hairstyle may be the closest she comes to realizing her dream – a Colette isolated by her gesture instead of liberated by it? I still want to believe it was my inability to help her, and not just an urge to flee from any part in her desperately imagined future, that prompted me to tell Cookie I had to get back to the ship.

Over the course of those years, I've often wondered when my ocean adventures began. Was it really with my father's many absences? What about my hypersensitive interest in maps of the Pacific Ocean? Or my love of books like *Robinson Crusoe* and *Treasure Island*? Even in retrospect, I can't wind the clock back to an exact moment or feeling. All I know for sure is that they ended on a clear and steamy morning in Apia, Western Samoa (Samoa, as it's now called) several weeks after I left Pago Pago.

That was the morning I visited Robert Louis Stevenson's hilltop grave, paying homage to the man who wrote *Treasure Island* long before he set eyes on the South Pacific (not that it mattered, since the book was actually based on the pirates of the Caribbean). On my way there, passersby often greeted me with cries of 'Peace Corps?'" 'Peace Corps?' But both the narrow dirt pathway that switch-backed up the hillside and the elevated gravesite itself were deserted and overgrown, the shadow of neglect deepest where the trees were closest.

Not too long ago I checked it out on Google Earth and, happily, everything looked trim and well-tended; the simple house-like shape of the grave now reminded me of a sculpture by Rachel

Whiteread. But what struck me then, and what strikes me still, is the short epitaph Stevenson chose for himself – his celebrated 'Requiem' – slightly misquoted on the bronze plaque:

> Under the wide and starry sky
> Dig the grave and let me lie.
> Glad did I live and gladly die,
> And I laid me down with a will.
> This be the verse you grave for me;
> "Here he lies where he longed to be,
> Home is the sailor, home from the sea,
> And the hunter home from the hill."

Needless to say, I can no longer read these words with anything like the romanticism that was typical of my teenage years. Far too many of the maps and descriptions I grew up with were colored by a colonial or libidinous hand. All too often the longing I projected onto them exaggerated the exotic. But as Thoreau wisely put it, everyone 'has to learn the points of compass again as often as he awakes, whether from sleep or any abstraction,' and I've been steering by a very different set of points – a very different set of feelings and abstractions – ever since.

I suspect I may have sensed this shifting course even then. I purposely postponed my visit to the grave until I was about to leave Western Samoa – as if I wanted the sweaty pilgrimage to be a symbolic coda or a goodbye of sorts. And so it was. Within a month, I returned to college in Ohio. Several years

later I moved to Brooklyn and earned an MFA.
Not long after that I joined Art & Language myself,
working closely with an Australian-born colleague
who later, it grieves me to say, drowned in the
Tasman Sea. Eventually I moved to Manhattan,
stopped making art, and began to write about the
American landscape.

Circumstances have left me landlocked ever
since – marooned on an island home away from the
sea. But the memory of my father keeps my reveries
current. When I watched his ashes disperse like
a thick fog in the waters off San Diego, I realized
that I would never be able to think of him again
without also thinking of the ocean: the two had
finally become one. Now I feel that each time the
East River rises it brings a particle of my father
with it; and each time it ebbs it carries him away
again. That, more than anything, makes me happy
to be one of Melville's wistful sentinels, standing
motionless for a few moments day after day, year
after year, on a promenade that's located thousands
of miles away from the full-fathomed waters of my
briny childhood. **H**

BIBLIOGRAPHY

Darwin, Charles. *Charles Darwin's Beagle Diary*. Edited by R.D. Keynes. Cambridge:
Cambridge University Press, 2001. [p. 38]

Melville, Herman. *Moby Dick*. New York: The New American Library, 1961. [p. 396]

Stevenson, Robert Louis. 'Requiem.' www.victorianweb.org/authors/stevenson/
requiem.html

Thoreau, Henry David. *A Week on the Concord and Merrimack Rivers, Walden, The Maine
Woods, Cape Cod*. New York: The Library of America, 1985. [hard bottom: p. 400;
compass: p. 459]

Whitman, Walt. 'Specimen Days.' In *The Portable Walt Whitman*. Edited by Mark Van
Doren. New York: Penguin Books, 1977. [p.427]

SAINSBURY CENTRE

THE YEAR AHEAD – 2020

Art Deco by the Sea
9 February – 14 June 2020

Art Nouveau:
The Nature of Dreams
29 March – 13 September 2020

Nara to Norwich:
Art and belief at the ends of the Silk Roads
26 July – 18 October 2020

Grayson Perry:
The Pre-Therapy Years
18 October 2020 – 31 January 2021

Henry Moore | Bill Brandt
22 November 2020 – 28 February 2021

All information correct at time of printing
Photograph: Pete Huggins

Sainsbury Centre
University of East Anglia
Norwich
NR4 7TJ

www.sainsburycentre.ac.uk

FOLLOW US

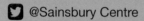 @Sainsbury Centre

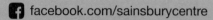 facebook.com/sainsburycentre

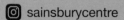 sainsburycentre

Restless
Creature

Restless
Creature

Restless

Restless Creature

by Emily Holt

I came across the text of *Ghost Story* years after
returning from Belfast. It had been long enough
that, sitting in the art library at the University of
Michigan, I was disturbed to read of a voiceover
in the 2007 short film by Willie Doherty. Walking
through the snow back to my friend's apartment in
Ann Arbor, I imagined locating a clip of the film
online: I pictured the moment when I would press
play as a movement akin to the way one might
approach a café where one is to meet an old friend,
or a past lover, one you haven't seen in years. Even
if the place the two of you once shared – the town,
the bed, perhaps – is only a dim room in your
memory, still it remains lit, and you approach with
a sense of return and surprise wound together.

Watching the clip at my friend's kitchen table that late spring day in Ann Arbor, still in my coat, I was shaken to realize that the voice-over has the compression, the visceral reach, of a certain kind of poetry. My sketchbook from Belfast refers to Doherty's piece with the barest details. The fact that the audio does not align directly with the video – a choice which might have lodged it further in the memory of another – enabled it to slip from mine. The visual, however, matches my notes and jumps between two scenes: a country path beaten down between tall grasses, and a back alley leading to a halting site with a clothesline and an abandoned car. The video opens and closes with the same image – right at the corner where you reach the car – always moving toward and away from its own beginning.

—

Nearly three years ago now, a man called my name as I was leaving a grocery store. I wasn't far from the university where I worked when I heard my name called with a touch of familiarity and urgency – the kind of urgency that beckons the crossing of new territories – and turned to see A., the man I had been with eight years ago when I moved to Belfast to work as a caregiver. On that late spring day in Seattle, we did the hurried and harried updating – him working at the large independent bookstore down the street, heading to Houston in the fall to get a PhD in English focusing, maybe, on representations of illness. I told him I had been accepted into Queen's in Belfast, also for a PhD, but that I wasn't sure if I would go. Money, the uncertainty of my mother's health, I said, affecting a shrug. A. once knew me well enough not to pry, and it seemed either distance or memory still held sway; he accepted my shrug.

I invited him to a multimedia exhibit on conflict in Northern Ireland that my partner and I were hosting that night. He came to the exhibit, asking at the end, a question about memory and violence. I saw him again in the bookstore a few days later. I ordered a book I didn't really need. I bought a card for my mother. We made plans to get a beer. And so, the spring before my mother died, there slowly arose an echo of pushing and pulling forces – the double bind that, uncannily enough, also existed right before I moved to Belfast and began to string together the series of images that come to constitute a life. To say that I eventually left Belfast for him is not simply a reliable cliché of love and distance. To say I left for him doesn't take into account how much more heavily the places weigh on me now. Some days, those memories of Belfast and Berlin are the only ones forceful enough to summon feeling or desire from the fog banks of grief, and I don't much mind that few may believe me when I say this focus on place doesn't lessen the human presence, the memory of one hand on another.

—

While the film's visual perspective only shifts between two scenes – a path in the country, one in the city – in the film's verbal arc violence rises swiftly, nearly triggering a sudden nausea, stronger on my second viewing. The violence Doherty reenacts is his memory of Bloody Sunday, the winter day in 1972 when British paratroopers shot 28 unarmed civilians in Derry, Northern Ireland.

That this reenactment is verbal and not visual leaves the viewer almost uncertain as to what their body has been subjected

That this reenactment is verbal and not visual leaves the viewer almost uncertain as to what their body has been subjected. The unseen speaker says they can see a faint river in the distance, a river invisible to the viewer. The speaker looks over his shoulder to find figures, shadow-like. The viewer maintains their steady gaze on a country path. The speaker remembers faces, rushing forward in a crowd, faces on a bright but cold January afternoon: men and women slipping on iced puddles, men, women, and children running for safety. A few run toward a wire fence and, finding themselves further trapped, try to scale it. As they do, a military vehicle appears, driving through the crowd, the fence, tossing bodies into the frosted air. When troops fire indiscriminately into the fleeing crowd, the speaker's voice cuts abruptly. And the viewer now eyes a back alley in a nameless city. The speaker can find no trace of the crowd. Another fence has been erected, he says, and a new building put in place, but still he wonders, 'Had it been absorbed or filtered into the ground or was it possible for others to sense it as I did?'

—

A few weeks after A. first called out my name, we met up for coffee, and it was soon apparent the extent to which it can be difficult to trust my senses when I am around him: to disentangle the words that pass between us from the aperture of our past. When he walked toward me, I was struck by his appearance – thinner, he wore his hair and beard longer, and seemed to have picked a pair of Carhartts and the hot pink tee-shirt of a cancer charity walk almost to counter my first impressions of him; years before he was always dressed in fitted jeans and nondescript black T-shirts. A. sat down across from me at the picnic table outside a bike shop not far from the university, and I mentioned I was reading *Death in Venice*. I asked how archetypal Gustav von Aschenbach was for a German man in his time. 'I want to know,' I said, 'because you can clearly tell he is headed toward a fall, toward passion, and who would want to read of this man who has lived his life so perfectly? Who has his perfect routine, his well-reviewed masterpieces but an unstated but felt fear of living?'

'He is lonely,' A. replied.

'Yes,' I said, though I know it sounded more like 'sure,' and A. repeated, 'He is lonely.'

I said 'sure', meaning it this time, wondering if he

got the subject of that sentence right, but A. moved on, saying Gustav was very archetypical, and that *The Magic Mountain* was Mann's rewriting of *Death in Venice*. Mann wasn't happy with what he'd said about passion and love and illness so tried again, making it about five times longer and opening his story with an 'unassuming' young man.

When A. mentioned the novel – the story of a young man who has gone to the mountains due to illness – I was startled, for it was this novel, unbeknownst to him, which had become important to me while I was in Belfast. That first line – 'An unassuming young man was travelling, in midsummer, from his native city of Hamburg to Davos-Platz in the Canton of the Grisons, on a three weeks' visit–' and then the description of the train, 'a narrow-gauge train,' and the 'steep and steady climb that seems never to come to an end' – had caught me as I stood that fall in a small, private library, overlooking a protest outside City Hall, holding the old paperback, wondering to what extent I still carried around with me the melancholy of one unassuming young man.

With that man now sitting before me, I said I worried that Mann had lost his insight about the need for passion, and I heard a voice in my head say, with more brass, *the need for love*, and A. repeated, though out loud, not in my head: 'he is lonely.'

—

There is something uncanny about reenactments. Sigmund Freud observed that even when actions are chosen, they seem involuntary. Even when low in risk, they have a driven quality. Tenacious. Freud named this recurrent intrusion of traumatic experience the 'repetition compulsion'. He first thought of it as an attempt to master the traumatic event. But he wasn't satisfied. It somehow failed to capture what he called the 'daemonic' quality of reenactment: the tenor of a woman walking down the street where she was attacked; a child reaching out toward the brother whose hand is raised; a young man kept in a closet as an infant later needing the hard walls of the psychiatric unit to calm his visions. Because the repetition compulsion seemed to defy conscious intent and to resist change so stubbornly, Freud despaired. There seemed nothing adaptive or life-affirming about the reenactments. In this despair, he created the concept of a 'death instinct'. Though most theorists have since rejected this explanation, the term 'death instinct' still occurs in psychological research, notably in research about

There is something uncanny about reenactments. Sigmund Freud observed that even when actions are chosen, they seem involuntary

post-Troubles trauma in Northern Ireland.

Most contemporary theorists now speculate that the repetitive reliving of the traumatic experience is a spontaneous, though often unsuccessful, attempt at healing. After Freud, Pierre Janet spoke of the person's need to 'assimilate' and 'liquidate' traumatic experience, which, when accomplished, produces a feeling of triumph. I am drawn toward Janet's water imagery, though to me water contains every association except triumph.

—

When I lived in Belfast, I visited Doherty's *Ghost Story* at the Ulster Museum as a momentary reprieve from the difficult day-to-day life of the care home where I worked. In those days, the dark, carpeted walls of the installation room could have been the edges of a bed, the catch of a pillow. They were days when it felt as if my head had begun to fall through itself, streaming through the previously comforting ideas of language and connection I had built as a literature and philosophy student. The fall and winter that I lived in Belfast, I often crossed the city, south to north, ranging a bit to the east, rarely to the west, to avoid this sense of falling, of tripping through a hall of visual and aural mirrors in a city made of walls and wire, with a river cutting through the center. I walked to avoid the knowledge that when my view of life had just began to expand, A.'s, it seemed, had began to contract.

He had just moved from the house we'd lived in with five other friends, that green house off 17th Avenue. He had moved back to campus, went to class, got a job that required little of him, but it was temporary, we both knew. The fact that he was to move to Berlin in December was the cause of our separation, and of its vague terms.

It was the evening before I was to take the train south to Carrickfergus that I received A.'s shortest email, the one that kept me awake. I paced my 6-by-8 foot attic room, veering toward and away from my computer at the small desk under the skylight, through which I could glimpse rows of chimneys and brick rooftops. The next morning, on the bus ride to the train station, passengers were forced to disembark due to a bomb threat, but I pressed on and my memory of Carrickfergus, renowned in tortured love songs of drinking and departure, is eclipsed by a single image: a dark line of northern hills encasing Belfast.

A. didn't have to write much for me to know what had begun, to know the height or the depth of where he had found himself. When we finally talked on Skype, it was an admission, almost a confession: unsettlingly quiet, the looping image of his uncle's gun in his hands. And abruptly the conversation turned – concerns about the necessity of days without me. *A test*, I wanted to say. *Necessity*, he said, our concerns shared via email and video, the circuits closed, offering just a hint of sweat, a touch of agony.

———

With Doherty's 2010 film *Segura*, for which the viewer must also sit in a dark installation room to watch grasses and stagnant water beneath an underpass occasionally lit by sodium light, it is more apparent than in *Ghost Story* that the viewer's perspective could be that of a security camera. Through these formal choices, Francis McKee sees Doherty evoking a 'folk-based security system', driven by the pervasive disbelief in one's perception of reality. In the disembodied quality of the camera movement in *Ghost Story*, Doherty disconnects the body speaking from the body moving. For McKee, this disconnection reveals Northern Ireland to be one of the first fully postmodern environments, where the British government used the Troubles and the disruption of democratic processes to justify the field-testing of new surveillance technologies. This fact often goes unacknowledged, McKee notes, because the region was socially provincial, a small place, one already full of the intimate, natural self-monitoring of people living closely together.

Ostensibly, I moved to Berlin to correct the initial post-college career detour I had initiated by accepting a job as a caregiver in Belfast

To turn to academic criticism in order to assess the long-term effects of Doherty's work on my psyche can, initially, feel as illuminating as considering Freud in a discussion about lost loves, sudden departures, the double bind. Ostensibly, I moved to Berlin to correct the initial post-college career detour I had initiated by accepting a job as a caregiver in Belfast. I believed that being immersed in the German language, rather than simply taking one evening class a week in Belfast, would surely prepare me for a graduate degree in translation. Yet when I turn to the experts, it is difficult not to admit

I was partly driven to leave Belfast to escape echoes
of what I'd wished to leave behind in the States:
the folk-based security of family, the dark pitch of
it. What I found in Berlin that spring eight years
ago was picturesque, wide-angled images of breezy
confidence – cutting and sexual. Now, when I am
in need of a similar reprieve from the intimacies
of family, I return in memory to the expansive
clothing-optional parks in Prenzlauer Berg and
Friedrichshain, where I sat alone in skirts and shirts
cut by my own scissors, and plowed through Don
Delilo's *Underworld*.

Before long, however, Freud's perspective
can become stifling, his world so singular in
its dimensions. There is something a touch too
textbook, too clinical about looking at my time
with A. from this perspective. It is to leave out the
awkward cursive, the heightened privacy of his
letters paradoxically lending a certain intimacy.
It is to leave out what both of us shed when, as I
made my way to Berlin, as he made his way around
Europe, we met, accidentally, in Prague, a city
to which neither of us had any ties. It is to forget
the automatic blinds of my hostel room – broken,
perpetually darkening the ceiling above us – and
how white the bed when they lifted.

———

I had remembered the movement of *Ghost Story*
as that of a body's pace, with all the slight jerks
of a handheld camera. Rewatching the clip, it

became clear that the camera, moving so fluidly over uneven ground, had to be on a dolly. What the viewer sees is what she would see if she were driving slowly down a country path or a back alley. But the speaker's voice reveals that what the viewer drives into is essentially invisible, an unspecified 'it' – the crowd, the soldiers, the guns simultaneously dissipating and mixing together, unable to be contained, seeping through every crack and fissure in the pavement. Midpoint in the film, the invisible matter, the remains of the bodies trapped against or thrown from the fence, become a tomb laying beneath the whole city. 'Not everyone can see them,' the voice admits. 'They inhabit a world somewhere between here and the next.' Whether these beings are a malevolent presence or a source of guidance ultimately depends on the viewer, who, sitting in the dark, feeling the slight vertigo of simultaneously moving forwards while sitting still, does not doubt the speaker when he says that the unnamed presence is now plural, is now corporeal: 'They move between the trees. Caressing every branch. Breathing, day and night, on every flickering leaf. They are restless creatures...'

———

As rush hour began and the sun started to fall behind the buildings off Broadway, A. switched the conversation slightly – laughing in his way about how it's odd to read Mann write about individuals in a sanatorium for TB, given that it is now so manageable an illness. With a chill in the air, thinking of my mother and other, seemingly manageable illnesses, I began to feel on display, as I had earlier, waiting for him, my bare shoulders warming in the sun, and so I let him keep the conversation away from all the uncertainties that her illness brought – where I would be living, whether I'd be studying, or still working. I let him continue to talk about how he learnt to speak English differently when he was teaching it in Germany. I thought of Susan Sontag's observation that it is passion that brings about the collapse of all that has made Gustav von Aschenbach 'singular'. So too did I threaten to bring about the collapse of all that made A. singular. For as I approached winter in Belfast, he was just

As I approached winter in Belfast, he was just beginning to become something ... and as long as I was there ... he would waste away

beginning to become something, he felt, and as long as I was there, beside him or at the end of his emails, he would waste away. If he didn't master German. If he couldn't feel the cheekiness, the joy, in the lyrics to *Blister in the Sun*. If he couldn't feel her tongue. Any other her. When I see him all these years later, I almost want to ask – *Did it work differently, her tongue?* Accustomed to those umlauts, the slight upturn at the end every sentence? Did it know better how to hold back? And was there passion in it still? With others, I would trust the answer, by necessity, to be yes.

———

In the text of *Ghost Story*, the arrival of a clear, defined self is tied to the arrival of a photograph. It is in a 'small, black and white newspaper photograph' that the speaker recognizes the face of a friend, murdered, the body discovered on 'an overcast Sunday morning.' Doherty knows that the personal does not rise, but sinks toward the stomach: the disbelief of encountering the one you've loved, dead, in the newspaper. It soon becomes clear that the speaker, retracing his steps along paths and streets he once avoided, must confront this absence: 'He was waiting for me as I always feared he would, emerging from a scorched corner...'

In the film's verbal score, this 'scorched corner' tips into another, morphs into the memory of shapes and colors from a television screen: 'The outline of a car silhouetted against a grey sky [...] A detail of the interior grey checked fabric, an oily stain, a cassette player.' And this car becomes another, appearing, it seems, from nowhere, the driver's face hidden by twilight and evening. The driver's singular face blurs into a multitude of faces: from photographs, film clips, from the voice's own closed-circuit memory. As the images enter our ears through the trained, near-crackling voice, pausing on each line break, they crystalize. In each silence, we imagine the stillness between frames, though our eyes have not left the path, the monochrome of grass, ditch, and sky.

—

Each time A. and I have met up since that day in spring, I have been highly conscious of the hour in which we meet, of any implied associations as day tips toward evening. When we were together, evening was the start; now, it is rush hour. As cars lined up along Broadway, I watched, from the corner of my eye, texts light up my phone: my partner, my mother, a close friend. I watched A. sweep his hair off his forehead and gesture to the book on the table before us, *Letters to Milena*, the book I was reading before he walked up to me. He's come to appreciate collections of letters between writers, he said, and I remembered how automatic or instinctual the air can feel between us, moving like a light wind. Watching A. play with the rim of his water glass, I recalled how, on one of my first days in Berlin, I saw him turn a corner on a hot day early in the spring, and how, from a distance, it seemed as if he had stepped out of death: the gun, the agony fallen from his hands. And so a pattern began in which it became hard to believe A. actually existed unless he was before me. Sitting there, touching the edge of Kafka's letters to his translator, A. admitted that he had started writing when he was with me; and I wondered if he expected me to string this fact to another, but he moved on, mentioning the letters of two writers who met only once in all the years of their correspondence – at the man's deathbed. And for no simple or clear reason, I thought of the extra mattress on the floor of the final room I rented in Berlin, where A. slept one night. I have

nearly recreated that night, fictionalized it with a
story in which a somewhat desperate woman follows
her lover to a small apartment in Prenzlauer Berg.
Their final night is one of thunderstorms, though
I know my final night with A. was not the week
I packed up my books and watched storms break
open outside the balcony. But in both the story and
in memory, a man sleeps on the extra mattress in
the corner of the woman's room. In both the story
and in memory, she lays down beside him, puts her
hand to his face. Restless, she knows night is merely
night. Restless, she knows the shapes on the floor
control the shadows on the walls.

—

There is no real winding-down in *Ghost Story*, no
apparent sense that the end is coming. Even if you
want to peer inside the car at the end of the path,
you sense you may not, and anxiety may rise. You've
been in a cycle of repetition, of reenactment, and
maybe you want to insist – *I have adapted. I can want*
not *to see inside the car.* Watching *Ghost Story*, it can be
easy to listen just to the cadence of the voice, which
is often hushing itself, letting the natural rhythms
of speech and thought move itself forward. It's easy
to ignore the actual words spoken and let the visual
pull you down the country path, the back alley.

Or at least it was easy for me, this highly visual
person, to do so. For I had forgotten the way the
speaker's tone becomes increasingly confident and
didactic as he summons the ghosts of his past:

'The daylight wraith takes on the likeness of a living person [...] someone who is in another place at the time of the appearance. They can even,' the speaker gestures toward the viewer, 'look like you.'

—

When we departed from the cycling café off Broadway to head back into our separate lives, A. and I agreed to stay in touch, perhaps even to see each other again. It was then, as we were about to separate, that the full heft of our separate lives rose up – that I live not alone but with a man I have been with all the years since A. and I were together. That my mother's illness was the sea above which I floated through apparently normal days answering phones, arranging events, taking minutes at the university which my partner, A., and I all once attended together. When A. and I vaguely referred to meeting up again before he headed back to Texas, I looked into the summer and didn't know what to see. I could not predict that in less than a week after seeing A. I would head down to California to hear that my mother had only months to live. I couldn't predict that in a few months, I would be the one who looked a bit like a wraith – fifteen pounds thinner, a chronic ache growing in my body that corresponded to the place where my mother's tumor took root. A. and I said goodbye lightly, we did not hug, we did not even touch.

Later that night, I lay in bed reading Kafka's letters to Milena, whom he came, it seems, to love. He is always imploring, beckoning, telling Milena that a letter from her 'removes several uncertainties. I see you more clearly,' Kafka writes, 'the movements of your body, your hands, so quick, so resolute it's almost like a meeting even so, when I then want to raise my eyes to your face, in the middle of the letter – what a story! – fire breaks out and I see nothing but fire.'

—

A. and I now write occasionally, the format mirroring his unspoken rules regarding contact: the occasional email giving way to the more honest handwritten letter, all signed with a single capital letter. Early on, I shared a link to Doherty's work – a film that ends with a car in flames in the middle of a field. A. said he appreciated that Doherty combined photo and sound – which is to say, that he used the medium of film. I knew A. was sincere, yet I was unable to shake the sense that for A., Doherty's imprecise focus and Kodochromic color palette must evoke uncomfortable associations with surveillance and intimacy. For his letters generally say little of his current life, unless I read them as I read a poem – unless I swallow whole the image of a man, sitting in the southwestern heat, caught between the croaking of frogs, the drip of traffic on the highway, and the drawl of the air conditioner. 'To read an image,' Alan Trachtenberg writes, 'is to write upon it, to incorporate it into a story.' A. resists story, and so I am left with a collection of unreadable images.

I believe he has one of me, an unreadable image, a photo taken the last time we met up. We were on a bluff, it was sunset, ships were passing in the water below. I had sat down on a bench to load a faster speed film into my camera. Working in the dim light with a digital camera, he kept shooting as I sat on the bench. He talked of wanting to return to film and, for a moment, I thought I saw a reversal of his usual dictum regarding the traces he and I leave behind, the negotiation of the space between our bodies. Though our correspondence leaves a physical trace, it is one which can be easily destroyed, easily burned. Even so, it's almost like a meeting – how, in the middle of a letter, an image overtakes and I want to raise my eyes to his face.

—

Those of us who have lost that person – that person without whom you could not keep on as before – know that part of you dies with them. After my mother died, and I continued to write to A., I asked myself, often – *Why does this matter, him once across from me, then not, his letters, then nothing for months?* It needn't. Each morning, an entire life rises around me. Yet each day is already day *without*, and loss a series of days in which you come to doubt the edges of your body. Yet you continue to appear in photographs. Others may think they know you, for you still live in a country and culture gorging itself on visuality. There are televisions, there are screens, there are even radios – but your dreams become visual as they never were before. You may dream in fiction, but the gist of it is always true, because your body is true. The dream may have risen straight from a film, a photo, but you have your own memory of a dazed woman huddling in a bright sunlit park, of a man turning the corner.

These days, when I can't sleep, which is not infrequent, I narrate the day in my head as I once did as a child in mass, addressing the stained glass windows on either side of the altar. Such a practice rarely leads me closer to sleep, but one blessing of grief is the fatigue that blows clear any delusions that forgetting will simply turn loss to water. When it seems most likely that I may wake a wraith, or may not wake at all, I lift my hand to a face; I cannot tell whose, but I lift my hand and so I sleep. I sleep and see nothing but fire. ◼

For the full text of 'Ghost Story' see Willie Doherty's *Requisite Distance, Ghost Story, and Landscape*, edited by Charlie Wylie, Dallas Museum of Art, Yale University Press, 2009, pp. 56-61.

On page 5, see Thomas Mann's *The Magic Mountain*, translated by H.T. Lowe-Porter, Alfred A. Knopf, 1955, p. 3.

On page 6, for a summary of Freud's discussion of repetition compulsion and Janet's of 'liquidating' traumatic experience, see Judith Herman's *Trauma and Recovery: The Aftermath of Violence—from Domestic Abuse to Political Terror*, Basic Books, 1997, p. 41.

On page 8, see Francis McKee's 'Smithereens,' in *Willie Doherty: Anthology of Time-Based works*, edited by Yilmaz Dziewior and Matthias Mühling, Hatje Cantz, 2007, pp. 19.

On page 10-11, see Susan Sontag's *Illness as Metaphor and AIDS and Its Metaphors*, Picador, 1989, p. 37.

On page 14, see Franz Kafka's *Letters to Milena*, translated by Philip Boehm, Schocken Books, 1990, p. 14.

On page 15, see Alan Trachtenberg's 'From Image to Story: Reading the File,' in *Documenting America, 1935-1943*, by Beverly W. Brannan, Carl Fleischhauer, Lawrence W. Levine, and Alan Trachtenberg, University of California Press, 1988, p. 45.

Notes from a Czechoslovakian Machine Shop

by René Georg Vasicek

'I want to be a machine,' Andy Warhol famously declared. Personally, I never wanted to be a machine. But God damn if I didn't feel like one when I was seventeen and turning steel on a lathe in my father's machine shop on Long Island. 'Piecework' is what my dad called it, although by the time the words got through his crooked yellow teeth and harsh Czech accent, it sounded like 'pisswork' – the mindless creation of thousands of identical metal parts.

My father often stood behind me, watching over my shoulder.

'Don't forget to tighten the chuck,' he once warned me, telling me how, when he was in trade school, a boy made a mistake. 'He turned the machine on and a piece of steel hit him in the head. Killed instantly. All of us watched his blood trickle down the drain.'

I worked on the lathe with a Marlboro cigarette in my mouth. Both hands preoccupied as it smoldered into my eyes. Vílem, the shop's foreman and elder statesman, observed me carefully. Himself a smoker, he walked over and slid his glasses down the bridge of his nose and peered at me with mock intensity. He did this whenever he wanted to impart machine shop wisdom. 'René,' he said in Czech, 'Either smoke or work — don't try to do both. If you want to smoke, step away from the machine and smoke. When you are ready to work, then work.'

We shot each other with powerful blasts of air from the pneumatic guns that dangled from coils above each machine. The air guns were used to blow away excess metal chips, but I doubt a machinist has ever walked the earth who could resist the temptation of blasting air at his *soudrůh* (or comrade, as we joked in the language of Czech socialism). After a particularly intense air gun fight, Vílem slid his glasses further down the bridge of his nose and again peered at me with his signature mock intensity. Vílem told me the story of how he once saw a man fall to the ground and writhe in pain after a comrade blasted him in the ass with a pneumatic gun. The intense air pressure ruptured the man's intestines and he died on the concrete floor within minutes. The lesson was understood: never place the nozzle of a pneumatic gun too close to a man's asshole.

Another time I was boring holes into aluminum blocks on a small drill press when a coil of metal suddenly wrapped itself around my fingers. Aghast at the sight of my own blood, I calmly turned off the machine and sat down on a stool... next thing

I knew, Vojta, a former woodsman in the spruce forests of Bohemia, was slapping me back into consciousness.

My father soon hired a Slovak named Fera. He had a prominent nose that protruded from a puffy face topped with ash-brown hair in tight curls. Fera chain-smoked and drove a dilapidated Mitsubishi compact, the ashtray overflowing with crushed yellow cigarette filters.

I do not know how Fera ended up at my father's machine shop. He had no experience operating a lathe or a milling machine

I do not know how Fera ended up at my father's machine shop. He had no experience operating a lathe or a milling machine. His English was primitive. But, then again, my father had a soft spot for men without mechanical skills, especially his countrymen — Bohemians, Moravians, and Slovaks — and he believed that the machine trade was learned by doing.

After work, Fera enjoyed sitting calmly and smoking with my dad in his office. I liked to sit with them. My father always had a six-pack or two of Molson Golden, Labatt's Blue, or Moosehead in the fridge. I got my father's bottle opener and popped open three bottles. We sipped the beer directly from the bottle and smoked our cigarettes. At seventeen, this was the only pub I could legally get into in America. It was my old man's pub, his own strange version of a Czech beer hall in the New World. My dad always sat at his desk, which was littered with blueprints, mechanical catalogs, a glass ash tray heaped with cigarette butts and a small free-standing plaque that read: *BOSS spelled backwards is double-SOB.* They told stories in Czech — once in a while I chimed in, but usually I just listened.

Fera blew his thoughts into the air in blue smoke rings. Each ring was a separate thought; its shape definite, dense and concentric at the point of creation, but nebulous and increasingly irrational as it rose toward the water-stained asbestos drop ceiling. I never knew what was really going on in Fera's head.

'I once made love to a Bulgarian girl,' Fera said out of nowhere. 'It was in a tent on the beach. I was vacationing on the coast. I can barely remember anything about her. I can't remember her name, the color of her hair, or even the color of her eyes. But I do remember that her feet smelled something awful, and it was all I could think of as we made love.'

My father erupted in uproarious laughter. I laughed too, but less so.

'And in the morning,' Fera continued, 'I was nude and alone. I looked outside to discover that someone had stolen my leather sandals in the night. To this day, I wonder if she stole them... and I can still recall that particular odor of her feet.'

I looked outside the window of the machine shop, and the parking lot was dark and empty. I didn't want to go out there, not just yet. It was in my father's office that all the men of the machine shop met before they went home to their families. It was an in-between place, neither work nor home, that some men prefer. Eventually we would each climb into our cars and drive home, our headlights barely penetrating the black void of the Long Island Expressway.

Fera discovered that I played tennis on the high school team. He said he played tennis himself, but that he hadn't picked up a racket in years. We agreed to meet the following weekend. He picked me up at my house in his Mitsubishi. We rolled down the windows, lit our cigarettes, and cruised west along Southaven Avenue in the smoke-mobile. Just as we crested the hill near Oak Street, we saw two pretty girls from my high school. I didn't know their names. They walked along the side of the road with their butts wrapped tightly in Jordache jeans.

As we drove by them, Fera turned to me and asked, 'How long do you have to go out with a girl before she will sleep with you?'

The question caught me by surprise.

I took a nervous drag off my cigarette and said, 'You mean me personally? Or do you mean in general?'

'No, not you personally,' Fera answered, 'but just in general — in America.'

'I guess that depends... it could be several months, maybe six months?'

'Hmmm... some girls in Czechoslovakia will make you wait a year, even two years.'

I told Fera to make a right onto Oregon Avenue, where we pulled into the parking lot of the tennis courts. Most of the courts were occupied, but we found a vacant one. On an adjacent court, two of my friends from the tennis team were embroiled in a vicious rally. After one of them hit a long ball that sailed into the chain-link fence, I introduced Fera to them. Fera smiled awkwardly and mustered a mumbled 'Hi' as he shook their hands. My friends were used to meeting the Czech émigrés and refugees from my world.

Fera's form was perfection rarely seen on public courts. It was not that Fera drove the ball particularly hard, although it was clear he could. Rather, it was that each groundstroke was simply beautiful

Fera and I stepped on to the court and started a casual rally, hitting the tennis ball back and forth, back and forth, back and forth. After a few rallies, I asked Fera if he wanted to play a match.

'No,' he said in Czech, 'I'd rather just rally. I haven't played in a very long time… I don't want to pull a muscle.'

My high school tennis coach pulled up to the tennis courts in his Chrysler LeBaron convertible, with the star of the girls' varsity tennis team. My coach's curiosity was piqued as he watched Fera and I rally through the chain-link fence. I knew what he was watching: Fera's form was perfection rarely seen on public courts. It was not that Fera drove the ball particularly hard, although it was clear he could. Rather, it was that each groundstroke was simply beautiful.

After rallying for about an hour, we got back into the dilapidated Mitsubishi and lit a cigarette. We sat in the parking lot in silence. Then Fera pulled out a newspaper clipping from his wallet and handed it to me.

'When I was seventeen,' he said out of nowhere, 'I entered a tennis tournament and was matched up against a relative newcomer: a fourteen-year-old named Ivan Lendl. Everyone called him *Nitěnka* (knitting thread) because he was so skinny. The results of the match appeared in a local Prague paper the next day. My father cut it out and saved it all these years. He sent it to me just last week.'

I glanced at the old and yellowed news clipping, and it read that Fera defeated Ivan Lendl in straight sets.

Fera started the engine of the dilapidated Mitsubishi. He put it into first gear and we drove off into a world in which Ivan Lendl was currently ranked the number one tennis player. **H**

The Royal Society
of Literature

RSL Awards & Prizes
now open for submissions

RSL Literature Matters Awards 2020

These Awards provide financial support to undertake a **new piece of writing or literary project**. Priority will be given to proposals which help connect with audiences/topics outside the usual reach of literature, and/or help generate public discussion about why literature matters.

Projects could include a piece or pieces of writing, a publication, an event, a production, on any subject and in any form, including (but not limited to) prose fiction or non-fiction, short stories, poetry, playwriting, screenwriting, graphic fiction, biography or travel-writing. The Awards are open to UK residents and there is there is a total of £20,000 available to be distributed across a number of projects.

RSL Christopher Bland Prize 2020

The **£10,000** RSL Christopher Bland Prize aims to encourage and celebrate older writers and is awarded annually to a debut novelist or popular non-fiction writer, **first published at the age of 50 or over** in the calendar year 2019. The 2020 Prize is open for publishers or agents to submit works by authors writing in English from the United Kingdom and the Republic of Ireland.

More information and guidelines
rsliterature.org

$tarting $alary

by Chris Jennings

Graphic Consultants sits in a business park of identical offices next to railroad tracks that drift off into the distance. The parking lot is strangely quiet, as if a plague had wiped out the working world.

The young man enters and walks up to the front desk. A squat black woman in flaming neon with large plastic hoop earrings and red acrylic fingernails sticks mailing labels on envelopes.

'Hi, I'm here to apply for the assistant editor position.'

She frowns.

'I'm sorry, what?'

'I think you have an assistant editor position listed in the newspaper?'

He produces said paper with the ad circled. She looks skeptical.

'Uh OK, just a minute.'

She picks up the phone, turns her head to the side, and whispers.

'Harold, there's a boy here about the ad. The editor position. I don't know. Do what? Now you *know* that's not my job. What?'

She pauses, looking put out.

'Whatever.'

She extends her arm and smiles broadly. A gold tooth gleams in the back of her mouth.

'Hi sugar, I'm Candy.'

'Chris. Chris Jennings.'

He shakes her small, plump hand.

'Go ahead and have a seat. We'll be right with you.'

She leaves in a wake of purple Lycra that jiggles when she walks. It's a shabby little lobby dressed in wood paneling with stained ceiling tiles and a carpet of orange fungus. Pictures hang unevenly on the wall depicting ducks frozen in mid-flight over reedy brown marshes. The furniture looks dusty and second-hand, faded from the fluorescent lights that sputter overhead. A mouse trap waits quietly in the corner.

He's interviewed long enough to know the signs of dubious employment. But he's living off the last of his student loans in a cockroach-infested apartment in San Diego with a Japanese-German girl, Yumi. Yumi recently reconciled with her gimpy ex-husband Mario, who runs an airbrush company with some drug-dealing on the side. They have a two-year old daughter who wakes up in the middle of the night demanding to watch *The Little Mermaid*. Yumi has been administering generous doses of cough syrup to calm the girl.

A man lumbers up, pink and obese with sagging jowls, balding orange hair, and a pronounced limp.

He wears a short-sleeve grey button-down that spills over grey baggy pants, wrinkled like elephant skin. He offers a thick stubby arm.

'Hey guy, nice to meet you. I'm Harold. You here for which position?'

Harold slurs his words.

'Assistant Editor? Well OK, let's get you an application. Candy, grab me an application, will ya?'

'I don't think we got none.'

Harold looks around helplessly.

'I told you we was out.'

'Hold on,' he grumbles.

Harold retrieves an application, blurred and faded from repeated photocopying. A previous applicant's credentials have been sloppily covered up with correction fluid. Harold hands him a dull, chewed-up pencil.

'Fill this out and lemmie know when you're done.'

It's a standard job application Jennings has seen in other offices. He lists his college job experience. Telemarketer. Arts writer for his college newspaper. A food delivery job that dressed him in a purple bowtie and cummerbund. It's the exact same information on the résumé he's brought with him, but he fills it out anyway, most recent first, in his best handwriting, and attaches the résumé carefully to the back with a pilfered paper clip.

'OK, step into my office,' Harold gestures with small circling motions.

The office is small and strewn with flow charts and graphs, statistical analyses, and demographic breakdowns. In the corners sit bales of newspapers, boxes of envelopes, postcards, and mass-mailing advertisements. Behind the desk, a small shredder spits thin slices of paper into a dusty black trash bag. There are plastic chairs and a fake leather couch leaking foam. Harold's desk is a forest of fast-food containers and soda cans, empty bags of chips, and candy bar wrappers. Harold squeezes sideways past the door jamb and collapses into a large rolling chair with a defeated sigh. He clears the desk with a quick slice of his hand.

Harold's desk is a forest of fast-food containers and soda cans, empty bags of chips, and candy bar wrappers

'Excuse the mess.'

Harold puts on a pair of cracked wire spectacles, furrows his brow, and peruses the application, running a ponderous finger over each line, mouthing the words. He glances briefly at the résumé, grimaces, pulls his face to one side, and puts a large hand on the back of his neck. An origami of folded flesh peeks out of the wet triangular shirt sleeve.

'OK, this looks pretty good. You just graduated. You have computer experience. Well, let me tell you a little bit about what we do here. See, we work with various businesses around the country to list their jobs in our newspapers, *The Daily Advertising Journal* and *The National Advertiser.* It's basically classified ads with a few pages of news for the older folks that like to keep up. We're looking for someone who can help our editor lay out the paper. We got about ten pages of news and the rest are job listings and advertisements. The guy we had went off and got married or something. So does this sound like the kind of thing you'd be interested in?'

'Absolutely.'

'Alright, well… you got the job. Be here at 8 am Monday.'

Jennings is shocked. After so many failed interviews, he had begun to wonder whether he would ever actually hold a professional job.

Monday morning, he waits outside the office with what look like Mexican laborers, strung-out heavy-metal musicians, Filipino gang members, high school drop-outs, elderly Chinese ladies, and skinny stubbly white men, one bender away from homelessness. The young men play-fight and push one another. The others smoke and talk. Jennings stands to one side and shifts his feet uncomfortably. He checks his watch. It's 8.25.

Jennings is shocked. After so many failed interviews, he had begun to wonder whether he would ever actually hold a professional job

'Where the hell is Harold?' Candy demands, rushing toward him.

Jennings shrugs, unsure if it's a rhetorical question.

'Damn that man, always late. Oh, here he is, finally!'

A rusted brown 1970s Cadillac screeches into the parking lot, spewing smoke and exhaust. Harold spills out of the car, out of breath, and hands Jennings a box of doughnuts, while he fumbles with the front door. Jennings peers dismally at his fingers, smeared with greasy chocolate from the bottom of the box. The employees enter and snatch up doughnuts without a word. Harold claps his fat stubby hands together.

'Alright everyone, hurry up and eat. Don't dawdle. Let's get to work now, chop chop!'

Harold looks flustered, as he sifts through piles of faxes, calendars, and sticky notes, blown across the desk like dead leaves.

'Harold, this is Chris Jennings, the new assistant editor.'

Harold stares at Candy, confused, until something in his face clicks.

'Oh, hey! Yeah, nice to meet you guy. Thanks for coming in. Let's see, what should we have you do today?'

'Don't forget, I got to take my son to the doctor's.'

'What? Your little boy sick again? OK I'll get this guy set up on the front desk while you're gone and break him in. What do you say, guy?'

'Sure.'

Harold lumbers out to the reception desk and gestures to Candy's chair.

'Well go ahead, have a seat. Have you ever answered a multi-line phone before?'

Jennings shakes his head.

'It's easy, when a call comes in, this button will start blinking. Push it down and say "Graphic Consultants, can I help you?" If any other calls arrive, these other buttons will start blinking. Say "please hold" and hit this red button. Easy peasy.'

'Now, this is important. Every once in a while a reporter will call, or someone from the FCC.

Don't tell them anything! You just say you don't know what they're talking about or "no comment." You got that? Be polite and hang up. That's all you need to do. Also, don't give out your real name. We get complaints about this or that every once in a while like someone got a bill in the mail for some advertising. You just tell 'em it's not a bill, it's a solicitation. Very important. See, we send these solicitations out to people to place ads in our newspaper, but sometimes they think they're bills and accidentally pay us. Well hell, if they do that, it's not our fault! We can't give the money back if we already ran the ad. But you tell 'em if they want us to keep running their ad, they can send in the amount listed in the top right-hand corner. Got it?'

Jennings nods, confused.

'OK, good. While you're doing that, you can stick these mailing labels on those envelopes.'

The envelopes contain fliers for a fabulous free grocery giveaway and advertisements that look remarkably similar to overdue invoices. The solicitations include a copy of the advertising listed in the *Daily Advertising Journal* or *The National Advertiser* and an amount owed, accompanied with an aggressive letter of non-payment. On the back of the bill, at the bottom, in faint yellow letters is a small simple disclaimer just as Harold described. *This is only a solicitation.*

Beyond the reception desk, a hallway leads back to a large cement garage with dim fluorescent lights and tall wooden tables where the workers sit. They talk and cut advertisements out of towers of newspapers stacked around them. Harold yells disparaging comments or tells dirty jokes. The floor is covered in newspaper scraps. An old radio with a broken antennae vacillates between country music and static. There's a ten-minute break when the employees smoke and eat and use the bathroom before Harold rounds them all up again with insults of encouragement and the whole process resumes.

After eating, Harold's head lilts back and forth on fatty deposits at the base of his neck and he falls asleep amongst the styrofoam containers and plasticware

For lunch, Harold sits in his car and devours double bacon cheeseburgers and bags of french fries, chicken tenders, and soda. He jokes he's got beers tucked under the seats for extra-hard workers. After eating, Harold's head lilts back and forth on fatty deposits at the base of his neck and he falls asleep amongst the styrofoam containers and plasticware, paper cups, potato-chip wrappers, beer cans, and old cigarette butts. Fossilized french fries and bent drinking straws poke out of cracks in the vinyl upholstery. Harold snores, jarred occasionally by bouts of suffocating apnea that shake the car. As lunch ends, he wakes instinctively and crawls out of the car, wearily admonishing everyone to get back to work. Then he puts on his bifocals and sits back down with the rest to cut up newspapers.

At the end of the day Harold announces it's time to clean up.

'Let's go boys and girls. Put away your things and let's get this place looking sharp. I don't want to see any scraps of paper anywhere. Put away those scissors. Move those newspapers into that corner. Throw those trash bags in the dumpster. Where's the new guy? Hey guy, I need you to vacuum the carpet and wipe down the bathroom. We trade off this job, so you won't have to do it every day. Vacuum's in the closet there. We got cleaners under the sink. It don't have to look real pretty, but straighten it up and all, you know? Don't forget to empty the trash. OK you guys, don't forget to punch out before you leave. We'll see you bright and early. If you're on time tomorrow, maybe you'll get doughnuts.'

We call this The Hole. It's kinda small, but at least it gets you away from all the riff raff. That's right, I'm talking about you guys

The next day, Harold shows Jennings his office.
'OK guy, let's get you set up. We call this The Hole. It's kinda small, but at least it gets you away from all the riff raff. That's right, I'm talking about you guys. Why? 'Cause you never work that's why. You're always chit-chatting and fucking around (excuse the language ladies). It gets pretty hot in here and we don't got any air conditioning, but there's a fan over there. I think it works. You might have to try the other outlet. I'd keep the lights off. You don't wanna know what's crawling around down there. We had the place fumigated about a month ago, but I don't know they did that great of a job. Goddamn cockroaches.'

Jennings shares The Hole with Rodney, the Associate Editor, whom everyone calls 'Hot Rod'.

Hot Rod has long limp hair and an endless selection of sleeveless Iron Maiden t-shirts. He learned graphic design and press board layout at a local community college. When Harold's not around, Hot Rod plays video games on an old black and white computer monitor and makes exploding noises with his mouth. Every day Jennings and Hot Rod download AP wire articles from an online bulletin board and use software to lay them out in newspaper format. They also scan in classified job ads from national publications like the *Wall Street Journal* and reformat them into their own Help Wanted section. But the majority of advertisements come from the warehouse workers who cut out ads from other newspapers and paste them onto Graphic Consultants press boards. Jennings' job is to print out news articles and lay these on the boards with the stolen classified ads.

Meanwhile, Harold and Candy coordinate a mass mailing to those same newspapers, which looks very much like an overdue bill, despite the obscure notice of solicitation. Jennings begins to understand that Graphic Consultants makes money by tricking businesses into thinking they've advertised in their papers. And based on the volume of angry and confused calls the office receives, he concludes that the only job college has qualified him to work is completely fraudulent.

He knows he can't stay. He knows this as he knows the schedule of trains that roar past the office. As he knows the stains on Harold's shirts or the greasy menu of the burrito truck that greets

them in the parking lot. Graphic Consultants hires
people who have failed in their everyday lives
(or never had much chance in the first place). He
doesn't belong here. At lunch, he walks along the
railroad tracks and wonders where they lead.

One day Harold calls him into the office.

'Hey guy, could I see you for a second?'

'What's up?'

'Have a seat. Listen, we're on a tight deadline
tonight guy, so I may need you to... errrghwww!'

Harold's face folds into a grimace, as he lifts a
hand to his sagging cheek.

'Goddamn it! My goddamn tooth! Where's my
gel?' Harold locates an exhausted tube of oral gel
in the mess on his desk and applies what is left
to his gums with dirty fat fingers. He sighs with
relief. 'Gotta keep rubbing this damn gel in my
mouth. Tastes like crap. Goddamn teeth are rotting
out. I tell ya, I'm literally falling apart here, guy.
You know I had a stroke a few months ago that
paralyzed half my body? Can you beat that? I can't
even move half my fuckin' face.'

Harold attempts to smile, which results in a
horrifying half-grimace.

'Can't barely even move this arm and my ex is
tryin' to get more money outta me... like squeezin'
blood from a turnip, I tell ya.'

'I didn't know you were married.'

'Yeah. Didn't last long though. I turn up one
evening. Driving home like I always do and see
all the lights off. She's supposed to be there, so I'm
thinking that's strange. I walk in and the first thing

I think is: Jesus we been robbed. There's nothing in the house. I mean nothing. And then I'm looking around for the phone to call the police and I realize there're no broken windows, the door's fine. Then I get it: Holy Christ, she's gone. She took everything and left. I mean, everything. She even took the batteries out of the fire alarm. The freakin' fire alarm. Probably had it out for me. Knew I'd fall asleep with a cigarette and burn myself up.

> **Holy Christ, she's gone. She took everything and left. I mean, everything. She even took the batteries out of the fire alarm**

'Oh yeah, I saw her again. She asked for money a couple months later and you know what, I gave it to her. Stupid. I haven't seen her in years. She didn't even come to the hospital after the stroke.' Harold runs a hand through his thinning red hair. White specks of dandruff dust the plaid mountains of his saggy breasts.

'On top of everything, I got the boss breathin' down my neck about these deadlines. I tell ya, the big guy and his attorney are makin' some serious dough in this operation, but do I see any of it? Hell, no. I barely make more than you, you know that? And I got years and years of management experience. Managed warehouses and docks, cleaning crews, construction sites, you name it.'

A nefarious crumb dislodges itself from the inside of Harold's nose and hangs precariously on to his left nostril. Harold scrunches up his face like an overstuffed rabbit and pinches it away. He rolls it between his fat fingers and flicks it aside.

'I don't know, I just don't know. Can't even afford to go to the damn doctor again. Poor bastard is never gonna get paid,' he chuckles. 'They got nothing good to tell me anyways. Stop smoking they says. Why go to the doctor if it's all bad news?'

You know I been smoking for over forty years. Can you believe that? Forty goddamn years. I started when I was eight

Harold pulls a pack of Marlboro Lights from his breast pocket, 'You smoke? That's good. Filthy habit. Once they got you, they got you. You know I been smoking for over forty years. Can you believe that? Forty goddamn years. I started when I was eight.'

Harold chokes briefly on a wad of phlegm. He grabs a wastebasket next to the desk with his good arm, holds it to his mouth, and spits into it.

'So, how we doing on the layout this week? Any problems? Good, good. So long as there's no problems. I don't like problems. Listen, tonight's our big crunch night and I may need you to stick around in case anything comes up. It doesn't happen often, but boy, I tell ya. We've had some real fuck-ups. Had people working 'till all hours of the morning. We gotta make at least thirty-five pages this week or the boss is gonna take it outta my butt.'

A cockroach scurries across the squalid topography of the desk. Jennings traces the insect's route and meets Harold's eyes. A moment passes between them; perhaps, an understanding. Without a word, Harold lifts his good hand and flattens the

roach with a leaden palm. Then sprays the hand
with a bottle of bright blue glass cleaner, wiping it
on his pants.

'Those guys in the back that fuck around all
day and never do any goddamn work, you let me
know if you see any of 'em loafin' around so I can
put my foot in their ass, OK?' One of the Mexican
workers exits the restroom outside of Harold's office.
'That's right!' Harold exclaims, 'I'm talking about
you Panchito! I swear, you give these 'spics an inch
they take a foot. So we gotta get this paper out early
today, OK? I don't wanna be here all night, capice?'

The needle-nosed company lawyer pops his head
into the office.

'Harold, I need to see you.'

'Be right there,' Harold grumbles.

'Now.'

Harold waves him off.

'OK, OK. Look, I gotta go. That's the boss'
attorney. We all gotta keep him happy or...'

Harold makes a slicing motion across his bulbous
turkey-waddle. He leans in close and lowers his voice.

'Hey, why do lawyers wear neckties?'

Jennings shakes his head.

'To keep the foreskin from crawling up their necks.'

Harold guffaws loudly before doubling over into
a wet rattle and lumbers out.

Jennings stays on for three more months before
packing his car and driving in the direction of
the train tracks. *Assistant Editor, Graphic Consultants*
would sit at the top of his résumé with contact

information he prayed no prospective employer would ever call.

'Oh yeah, Jennings, I remember that guy. Always showed up to work on time. Yeah, I'd totally recommend him, swell guy. Tell him I said hi, would ya?'

In an unexpected epilogue, years later, Jennings revisited the city of his lousy job prospects and spilled beer down some drunk's back in a crowded bar. The man became confrontational, insisting that Jennings, for some incoherent reason, doused him in beer on purpose. But there was something familiar about the drunk. Like someone he'd seen walking in the opposite direction every day, but never talked to. In a feat of connective memory, he realized that it was 'Hot Rod' Rodney, the former Associate Editor of Graphic Consultants.

> **The man became confrontational, insisting that Jennings, for some incoherent reason, doused him in beer on purpose. But there was something familiar about the drunk**

After some earnest convincing, an enlightened look spread across Hot Rod's face, as he recalled that karmic lifetime ago. He embraced Jennings in disbelief like an old army buddy back from the war. They reminisced about their former employer and Hot Rod told him that a few months after he left, the Feds came in and busted the whole operation. The workers showed up to find a giant padlock on the door accompanied by a government notice of foreclosure. The mastermind behind the whole operation was, of course, a business professor from Jennings' alma mater, who was now serving time for fraud. Rodney didn't know what happened to Harold and all the rest.

If Harold were still alive, Jennings imagines him sleeping in that rusted-out Cadillac in a business park of identical offices, snoring loudly amongst the tumbleweeds of fast-food wrappers. Until lunch time ends, when he wakes up as if on auto-pilot and staggers back to work. ∎

Thank You,

Penarth

by Amy Davies

I t's a cliché, being drawn to the sea, using it as both metaphor and a cure-all for life's problems and woes. But clichés come from somewhere. For me, the sea – and one particular stretch of it – has been both saviour and a release.

I spend most of my life in solitude, working as a freelance writer and photographer. Running to your own schedule can be fantastic, but there is a price for such freedom. Days, sometimes weeks, can pass without real contact with another human being. In the winter, with short days and darkness descending before the strike of five, the loneliness and isolation compounds itself. At times it becomes overwhelming.

I lived through many – too many – years hating September and October because they signalled what was soon to come. I spent the final days of summer clinging on to the last vestiges of daylight, yet unable to enjoy them. Feeling a dread for the winter, which, it seemed to me, threatened to drag on forever.

You've almost certainly never been to Penarth Beach. The small South Wales town of Penarth sits only a few miles outside of Cardiff, but even those who live local to it don't seem to bother too much with the beach itself. You can't blame them: the main attraction of the esplanade is the charming Victorian pier. You won't find miles and miles of golden sand – in fact, the beach is mostly pebbles and brown sludge.

At high tide, you'll find barely a slither of available beach. At low tide, the vast iron structure of the pier is revealed and, if you can navigate the unforgiving ground beneath you, sometimes it is possible to walk all the way around (but take shoes that you don't mind wrecking in the aforementioned brown sludge). One day I did just this, if only to see what the back-end of a pier looks like. I don't know what I was expecting, but a structure reminiscent of a multi-storey carpark certainly wasn't it. I had a precarious journey back, feeling at any moment as if the sand might give way and swallow me up.

One of my favourite activities is to stand directly underneath the pier. You can hear the sounds of people walking on the wooden boards above, while at the same time you are surrounded by nobody at all. The huge, barnacle-encrusted sturdy beams that have towered over the beach for more than 120 years seem all the more glorious from beneath. When the light is just right they cast the most curious shadows. Pools of water house glistening seaweed, as well as paw and claw prints from the dogs and seagulls – the only evidence of other visitors.

The Bristol Channel has the second highest tidal range in the world, a fact that I never tire of reporting to anyone who will listen

Another favourite pastime is to watch the tide. The Bristol Channel has the second highest tidal range in the world, a fact that I never tire of reporting to anyone who will listen. Imagine it: you can arrive at Penarth when the tide is practically crashing up against the sea wall, and an hour later it will be barely lapping at the outer edges of the pier.

Growing up right in the middle of the UK, a visit to the seaside was once a rare treat; something that I only ever associated with special trips, holidays or other unique occasions. Now, I live within a 15-minute drive to the beach and can visit whenever I feel like it.

I was never formally diagnosed with Seasonal Affective Disorder, but I certainly experienced some of the syndrome's classic symptoms: depression, lethargy, difficulty getting up in the morning, and difficulty concentrating. I knew it would take a serious shift in mindset to get rid of it, but I was determined. For me the solution lay in that sludgy, pebbly beach that I am so lucky to live just minutes away from.

During the winter months I take advantage of every sunny day. Having no set schedule, I can, within reason, do this with ease; another thing to be grateful for. Such days may be few and far between but, when they arrive, I do my very best not to ignore them. Getting out and standing on that beach in the freezing cold but oh-so-bright and brilliant sunshine – most of the time with only my dog for company – brings a kind of clarity that, without fail, lifts my mood. If the subsequent days are grey, cold and miserable then that's OK: I just look ahead to the next beach trip.

As a photographer I take hundreds of images every week, but somewhere along the way I lost the love of capturing pictures just for the sake of it. That's something else I've rediscovered in Penarth. I might have thousands of pictures that will be of little significance once I'm gone, but they exist as a record of a place that I will be forever grateful to.

Thank you, Penarth. **H**

Double page
spread,
full colour –
£350

Single page,
full colour –
£200

Half page,
full colour –
£120

Single page,
b&w – £150

Half page,
b&w – £70

To take advantage of the above rates and advertise
with Hinterland, or to discuss sponsorship
or other collaborations, please contact
Andrew Kenrick: hinterlandnonfiction@gmail.com

HINTERLAND

Hinterland publishes the bestselling
authors you know and love, as well as
the fresh new voices of tomorrow.
Our readers are intelligent,
creative and curious.
If this is the company you'd like
to keep, consider advertising
your product or service with us.

At the Ambassadors

by George Szirtes

Saturday night at The Ambassadors. I am sitting on the raised part of the floor, at a table, with a basket full of chips in front of me.

Larry Magnolia has poured himself into his gold suit. Mal Gallicott is snarling in his leopard-skin lapels. And what does Larry say? He is pointing at the gaffer tape on the mat.

You want tawdry, ladies and gentlemen? We give you tawdry.

You could dance, you could go out for a decent meal or drive out into the country in search of a fairground, looking for the acrid taste of raw nostalgia. And you could find it. It doesn't have to be real. Nostalgia is happiness at the edge of language, a tip-of-the-tongue elusive flavour. You could even find it here if that was what you wanted. Nostalgia as tawdriness worked into a glossy routine. It's not what they want, though. Not exactly. What they want, what they have become addicted to, is truth; and truth precisely in this guise.

A boy in a white mouse outfit runs about the room. He has a slight paunch and a long, ratty tail. A man at one of the tables pretends to pick a fight with him: the mouse hides behind a pillar and flaps at him with his little hands.

An elderly man sits three chairs down, his face impassive, immobile. A couple opposite with the same statuesque stillness. They're dotted here and there. Their faces have slipped and settled.

The wrestlers enter the ring. The first has a sweet, effeminate softness in his body. He is known as Boy. He is neither particularly tall nor particularly wide. He wears his hair mullet-style. He looks like a boy on the market, nothing more, but he plays hero in a Union Jack costume. The softness and ordinariness is what Larry Magnolia is picking at. But the irony is more complex than he knows. It's there in the costume. We are Brits, the costume says. We are not enormous yankee myths projected onto glossy limbs nor are we Braveheart leading a bunch of brittle, vainglorious Scots. But just in case you're thinking you can mess with us, we carry this smelly old lineament bottle full of irony, and should it come to that, we'll smash your fucking face in with it.

His opponent for tonight, the heel of the contest, is Todd 'Skull' Harte, nineteen stone and rising. Skull wears black and has a small but engaging repertoire of sneers: the sneer contemptuous; the sneer threatening; the sneer puzzled for when he's thrown; the sneer twinkling for when he has inflicted pain on his opponent; and the sneer jovial, which quickly shades into the sneer ironic that undermines the rest.

And I tell you what. It frightens me, says Larry Magnolia.

Nineteen-stone Skull and twelve-stone Boy are father and son.

Father charges at son. Throws him once, throws him twice. Quick, like that. Holds him in a standing headlock, then applies a double wrist-lock and head scissors. You don't want to hurt your lad too much. Throws him again. The Boy goes hard on his back. This round consists entirely of Skull playing rag doll with him. So does the next. If you were coming for the first time you'd wonder how it was that Boy survives, especially as he has already been thrown out of the ring twice. But when you get used to the rhythm of the thing, you see there is less contact than you imagine. The choreography is fine. You get a body slam and the arms go down hard to make a wonderful boom that makes you think your vertebrae have just impacted with your sacrum so you're fused forever, you and the mat below you. But give it a head-shaking three or four seconds and you're up delivering a forearm smash or a flying mare or smashing your opponent's head against the ropes. Your timing has to be right.

By the third round things have changed. Boy spins away from his father, leaps over him, rolls under his legs, bounces off the rope and tips him over, so both his shoulders are touching the ground. That's one fall to Boy. Hero: one, villain: nil. Perhaps the twist in the proceedings has come a little early for you? Myself, I don't think it's too bad. In fact there's nothing shamefully below par here, not by today's standards. The moves are good, the timing's pretty well on the spot. As for the plot, the narrative if you like, it has a certain flow and tension.

The girls in the audience fist the air. One middle-aged man at a table takes Skull's side and encourages him, but Skull loses this one because the story demands it. He returns to the dressing room.

The fat man slinks back, a whale moving through water, which divides before him.

To tell the truth I am not strictly a fan of the game as it is now. I seem to have wandered into it as if by mistake. While it's true that I am by no means indifferent to sport, I have never much liked the more bruising forms of physical contact.

There lies the enigma. Perhaps the truth is that I don't know what precisely draws me to it, but I do feel there is something in all this: a voice, a smell, a kind of weight. And the wrestlers I am watching, those I do not understand – because, after all, other people, all other people, are impossible to understand, but especially those whose life is spent in quite a different sphere – these figures are a kind of torch, an amulet to guide us through to the other side.

Perhaps they too feel the oddness, grotesqueness, comedy, power and lyricism of the world they have lived through, but if not, their very being may be capable of amplifying it for us, as we move with them in their own eternal present tense, hiding ourselves in them, like a blind spirit seeking light in the eyes of others.

Here come the midgets, the obese, the painted, the women, the managers with their baseball bats and folding chairs, the mice, the rabbits, the thugs, the dead, the murderers, the heroes and the gods.

Think of the violence, ladies and gentlemen, simpers Larry Magnolia. Think of the smell. I wouldn't touch them with a bargepole, would you? Would you madam?

A boy rushes on with a bargepole and Larry hands it to a woman who has raised her hand. **⊞**

Photograph of Magda Szirtes

IN CONVERSATION WITH
George Szirtes

By Helen Szirtes

There were three stories about my grandmother
Magda, whom I sadly never met, that formed my
understanding of her as a child. All three involved
some remarkable or awful coincidence, some twist
of fate, that gave them an almost mythical feel. First
was the story of her death, which followed a suicide
attempt, when the ambulance taking her to hospital
was delayed by a crash; the second came from my
grandfather, who would tell me how, on a night
off from forced labour, far from home and years
before they met in Budapest and fell in love, he had
danced with my grandmother at a social event. But
it was the third anecdote that, above all, defined the
story of her and whispered through everything else
I heard or sensed about her as a person. It was the
story of a betrayal, a theme that I now realise ran
through her life. It led to her deportation, and the
concentration camps, to a dark blot in her history
that we can never really know. She survived, though,
and went on surviving for as long as she could,
holding the children she had afterwards fiercely
close, fleeing the Hungarian Revolution in 1956
and landing in England with only her most precious
things: her family and a small case of photographs.
   How glad I am that she did, of course, for I
would not be here otherwise. Nor would my father's

book about her, *The Photographer at Sixteen*, which could not exist without that case of photographs. Those three stories, and so many extraordinary others borne out of that particular period of history are all recorded in the book. Reading it is as close as I, or anyone, will ever get to meeting her, and actually, that feels pretty close.

The Photographer at Sixteen is my father, George Szirtes', first book of creative non-fiction after forty years of publishing poetry, translations and essays. He is a poet first and foremost, though he trained as an artist, and everything he writes is informed by that dual sensibility: by the desire to capture the otherness of a thing by rendering it through a mix of observation and invention. The book is a portrait of my grandmother, his mother. It opens with that first story of her suicide and death, working back through the tides of memory and then history to the moment where, in an allusion to an Anthony Hecht poem imagining life as a film played in reverse, his mother, as a diver, has emerged back out of the water and stands magically again at the top of the diving board.

I met with my father to talk about the book and how he approached a subject that is at once so personal to him and yet so mysterious.

—

Helen Szirtes: You've been very active on social media over the last ten years or so, using it as a journal and poetry sketchbook but also posting reflections on a range of subjects; anything that's been simmering in your mind. It feels in a way like you've been building up to writing a book like this, and that your output on social media has contributed to your readiness to do so. How long had *The Photographer at Sixteen* been brewing, and why this first crossover into creative non-fiction now?

George Szirtes: In 2015, a writer friend insisted I should tell my mother's story. Two hundred pages in six months, he told me. I'd written quite a few poems about her but that was long ago. So I said all right, and it was only once I had promised that the thought of 'how' arose. I regarded the book as a kind of commission. My best writing has sometimes been the product of a 'commission'. My experiments in social media had given me some confidence in addressing a general rather than purely literary audience. They also sharpened my ear by teaching me the balance between poetry, prose poetry and the poetics of ordinary prose.

HS: When I first read a draft of the book, I knew it was something special, unusual not just in how it uses photos as jumping-off points or tells the story backwards, but in the way it openly analyses the whole process. I worried about publishers being wary of a book that defied easy categorisation.

GS: Yes, it is a hybrid kind of book, a memoir moving into a biography of my mother and, in the third part, into something different from either. All memoirs are products of memory, of course. Mine is different in two possible ways, neither original in itself but maybe striking when taken together: the telling backwards (other people have told stories backwards); and its constant questioning of memory, to what degree it is reliable and how much of it is invention and hearsay – a mixture of things other people have told us, things we think we remember and things we may be reasonably sure have actually happened. It ponders how far memory itself is a construction, and how far it might be necessary to construct the figure of my mother, not so much as a subject but a presence.

HS: I suppose by focusing on the process of construction, you found a way to write about something incredibly personal without getting tangled up in it. The voice is always looking for more than feeling, but is also able to see beyond what a historian or biographer would, because you are her son. I think it's striking for its honesty and its control, always respectful, generous, humble, curious – there's hardly any judgement, either of your mother or your younger self. But there must have been times with Magda when your emotions were harder to keep in check.

GS: It's interesting that all of the book reviews make different character judgements of her. One says, 'What a difficult person', another, 'What a brave person', yet another, 'What a beautiful person'. One reviewer goes so far as to say he could have fallen in love with her! And to tell the truth, I think they are all right in their way. I wanted to avoid being sentimental or sensationalist, because there were, after all, events in her life about which it would have been all too easy to be sentimental or sensational. There were the concentration camps, the leaving of her home town at an early age to pursue a career in photography, the escape at night from Hungary following the uprising of 1956, and the becoming a refugee in England. There was an epic quality in her life. But my priority was to understand her in the way I never did as a child or adolescent. I'm not sure I understand her even now.

HS: How could you, though, at the time, when you didn't know what she'd been through?

GS: It's true that, like many others of her generation and broad experience, she didn't talk much about her life. It was really the recorded interviews with my father that I began almost immediately after her death, chiefly as an attempt to distract him from his own grief, that opened up her history to some extent. My task, as I saw it then, was not to ask specifically about her: the interviews were about his life, starting from the very beginning, but she was, of course, bound to come into the story at some point, and when she did, it was in some detail. It was the first time I could think about her life before children – that is to say my brother and me – and also, in so far as my father knew, of her life as a child and young adult. Those are important stages in the book's reversal of chronological order, and the reason for the three-part division. In the first she is my mother as I remember her, and is referred to as 'my mother'; in the second (which relies heavily on my father's account and involves her experience in the camps) she has a life independent of us and is referred to by her given name, 'Magda'. And in the third she is a mysterious child I know only from some studio photographs, from odd scraps she herself divulged, and anything else I could discover, which was little considering her entire family was wiped out in the war. In all three parts of the book I treat anything I learn as provisional, even if it is someone as close to her as my father who is telling me. The further I go back, the more I have to take guesses, until eventually I need to speculate on a gesture or expression in a photograph, and to have imagined conversations not only with her, but with the studio photographer. The project is a bit like a detective story in that it begins with a body then tries to work out how it got there. But there is nothing absolutely certain in it. I can only conjure a lost presence that I have to assume is hers. Hence the constant element of doubt in the book, which is, essentially, about what you can know and what you can't, and about what you are doing by speculating.

HS: I know from your past forays into novel writing that you weren't at home with that form of storytelling – I remember that you found it hard to engage with the mechanics of plot, the business of moving the pieces from A to B. This, on the other hand, is a story you wrote fast and, I think, instinctively. Was that because the subject was so well known to you or because inventing the truth is just more natural to you than inventing fiction?

GS: That has been my experience, yes. In this case there was a real life to be following, which meant I didn't have to invent story and plot. Inventing events and peopling them with invented figures is difficult for me. Completed stories with their complete arcs are a problem. I don't fully believe in them. My task was to follow the clues and to construct a truth I could actually believe in. Poets invent metaphors; they don't invent stories. And I think that's what I'm doing.

HS: Which suggests non-fiction can be every bit as close to poetry as fiction.

GS: I think all kinds of writing can be close to poetry. I love writing that gazes at things and is moved more by phenomena than by stories. The best nonfiction gazes at the world with a certain disinterest while entertaining a range of complex emotions that it looks to navigate as honestly as possible. Poetic writing doesn't mean pretty writing, it means being precise, almost forensic, yet slightly dazed by everything.

HS: But that being dazed – does that not suggest the antithesis of precision?

GS: The task is to work *precisely* through the haze. The haze never quite goes, nor should it. We know there is something perfectly precise in there and that we have to use all our concentration to approach it. I suspect it is the object itself that generates the haze. This book doesn't solve anything. It works its way through the subject's own haze. My mother is that haze.

HS: So it doesn't solve anything – there is still a mystery to Magda, as there is to everyone – but I wonder if a line has been drawn under the subject of your mother now. She's been such a haunting presence in your work. Do you think to some degree her ghost has finally been able to pass through the walls of your imagination?

GS: Ah, you're referring to my 1988 poem 'Metro'.

HS: Yes, the part where you imagine Magda hanging up her coat after work and walking through the wall of the apartment to join the damaged statues on the outside – those allegorical figures you find on many Budapest buildings. One reviewer described the book as a monument to your mother: do you think that by restoring her through memory and invention to a position of innocence, where she is no longer 'broken statuary', her spirit can be laid to rest and you can move on?

GS: I don't think there is ever a process of complete healing, of complete recovery. I don't think she has emerged from the wall unbroken but at least she is working her way through it. When I first went back to Budapest in 1984, it was a little like re-establishing contact with her as well as myself. The city's history was also her history. Can her spirit be laid to rest? I'm seventy now. Most of my effort when young was to get away from her, not to be under her direct influence, not to be a kind of animated puppet, not to be the vehicle of her realisation. Will I have the opportunity to return to her? Not immediately.

HS: My favourite part of the book is the third section.

GS: Mine too.

HS: You're looking forensically at these five early photos from Magda's childhood, sometimes conversing directly with her as you make observations and guesses, sometimes stepping into the shoes of the studio photographer. And interspersed are snippets from her letters that wrench one from the pretty child with a Minnie Mouse bow back to the desperate mother leaning towards an exit from life. It's where the beginning meets the end, in a sense, and it's profoundly moving. You seem to be holding each other to account, in order to come to some kind of reconciliation. Words like 'I love you' and 'I'm sorry' are never exchanged, but they're just under the surface.

GS: I think what I have against sentimentality is that it's not true. It is the rounding up of something that is never going to be fully rounded. And the word most frequently sentimentalised is 'love'. That doesn't mean that the thing itself doesn't exist, of course, it is just that the word fulfils so many functions that it is far too precious to be applied in every case. Love has to be borne out and I hope the book has a decent go at bearing it out. My mother staked so much on love: 'You will never love me as much as I love you,' she said, and meant it. But love in such terms is both gift and demand, and it is all but impossible to sort one from the other. I never once thought I must write a book to show how much I love my mother. I very much wanted to avoid that. Don't sentimentalise. Declarations of sentiment might not be true.

HS: In what sense would they not be true for you?

GS: In that I wasn't sure that what I felt was love, not at least as she meant it. I understood that her love came complete with conditions and demands, and that it could be stifling. I spent my adolescence trying to resist it, and she found that resistance enormously frustrating and painful. But it wasn't intended to hurt her: it was intended to preserve me. I can't remember ever thinking, Oh, I love my mother. I really don't. I can see why I should have and I can see that although I probably never once thought it, I probably did. But that was her business: love? Oh, she deals with that. *She fires it at you like a bullet.* Thinking that is a source of guilt throughout the book.

HS: Did these complex feelings make writing the last section harder? You say it's your favourite section too, so perhaps it was easier. Or just different?

GS: Different. But in some ways better, because I was working closer to my poetic instincts. I think of the last part of the book essentially as a kind of poetry. It does what poetry does. It *realises*; it makes real an imaginary situation as, in this case, mediated through photographs. Photographs are magical objects. They are, as Barthes says, *memento mori*, symbolic of our mortality, but they are also spells to conjure us across time and to enable us to confront it. There's one photo where I think she looks a bit crazy, and another, the one on the cover, where I think, *That's a very pretty young woman who knows she is*. She is detached from me. It's like that passage in the book where she dances in the snow. She becomes an independent other, someone I don't fully recognise. It is a shock. When I look at those very early photographs of her they strike me as images of time that are, paradoxically, wildly out of time, wherein she has become the out-of-time creature with whom the book has to form a working relationship.

HS: Perhaps it's your wariness of sentimentality that makes you, as a writer, more comfortable with 'you', 'we' or 'one' as subject pronouns than 'I'. But here you're not only the teller of the story, you're a character in it. You can't avoid 'I' altogether. I'm interested to know what you think the reader might learn about you from this book.

GS: That's an interesting question. Obviously the book is about my mother, but it's a memoir in the first part, and while I'm absent as a character in the second, it is inevitable, I suppose, that it will be read through my relationship to her, that is to say in the light of the first part. In other words I cannot be perceived – nor am I – a fully objective outsider. Readers might detect a certain temperament at work. They will understand that I'm a poet and that I have a deep interest not only in the subjects of specific photographs, but also in what a photograph actually is and can tell us. Readers might also note a certain kind of approach to the subject – a desire, if you like, to stand clear but not out of touching distance. They will take the narrator's voice and choices as mine and those will strike them this way or that, depending on who they are. It's like with the reviewers who have different views of her: I suspect I am one of them! That multiplicity suggests something about me, or her, but I'm not sure what. But what do I learn of myself? Very little that is new. I seem to be the same complicated blend of doubt and resolution, a slightly detached hoverer over the world with all its potential and historical terrors, a creature of language. I am not sure what else readers can conclude about me. No more than I can about myself, I suppose.

The hardcover edition of The Photographer at Sixteen *is out now from MacLehose Press.* ◫

The Real Story

DEVELOPING CREATIVE NONFICTION
AND THE ESSAY IN THE UK

The Real Story is a Manchester-based writer development project and online journal devoted to promoting the form of creative nonfiction writing in the UK. Funded by Arts Council England, we provide workshops, mentoring and a publishing platform for both established and emerging creative nonfiction talent. We're always looking for personal essays and pitches, so head over to therealstory.org/submit and send us something wonderful.

LOTTERY FUNDED

Supported using public funding by

ARTS COUNCIL
ENGLAND

Like what you've read?

Look out for the fourth issue of Hinterland, on sale February 2020. Better still, sign up for a subscription and get our next batch of stand-out writing delivered direct to your door, desktop or tablet.

Annual print & digital subscription £34
Four issues, saving £6 off list price

Annual digital subscription £20
Four issues, saving £4 off list price

Subscribers also enjoy the benefit of being able to submit their writing to Hinterland free of charge.

Visit our website to subscribe:

www.hinterlandnonfiction.com/subscribe